11 95

THE CANDLES ARE STILL BURNING

THE CANDLES ARE
STILL BURNING

*Directions in Sacrament
and Spirituality*

Edited by
MARY GREY
ANDRÉE HEATON
and DANNY SULLIVAN

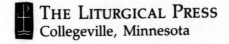
THE LITURGICAL PRESS
Collegeville, Minnesota

Published in North America by The Liturgical Press, Collegeville, Minnesota

Published in Great Britain by Geoffrey Chapman, a Cassell imprint

First published 1995

ISBN 0–8146–2392–1

The extract from Brian Keenan, *An Evil Cradling* on p. 17 is used by permission of
Hutchinson Books Ltd.

The extracts from Adrienne Rich, 'Natural Resources' and 'Contradictions: Tracking
Poems' on pp. 13 and 18 are used by permission of W. W. Norton and Company, New
York.

Typeset by York House Typographic Ltd, London

Printed and bound in Great Britain by Mackays of Chatham plc

Contents

Introduction

CHRISTIANE BRUSSELMANS influenced the lives of numerous people on a world-wide level with a vision of the sacraments which touched the deepest roots of their human experience. It was a *uniting and integrating* vision, which integrated reflection on lived experience with the liturgical, celebratory dimension and both of these within the hope of a renewed and revivified Church which listened and responded to the breath of the Spirit. It was *uniting* in the sense of uniting theology with its roots in prayer and contemplation and uniting liturgy with the active apostolate. This was no narrow ritualistic understanding of the sacraments, but deeply theological in drawing on the sacramental vision of the early Church, and deeply ecclesial in locating the sacramental heart in the local church community. It was a vision profoundly sensitive to culture – at home equally in Europe, North or South America or the Caribbean. She was particularly sensitive to the Puerto Ricans in Harlem. But it was with children that it all began. As she herself told the story: her father was very concerned about the faith education of his (then) 46 grandchildren, so simply told Christiane to study theology and take care of their religious education. Thus was Christiane, a guitar player and poultry-keeper, thrust into years of traditional theology at the University of Leuven, Belgium and the Institut Catholique in Paris, rich formative years for her, when this integrating vision enabled her to make the needs of children in their family situation the touchstone of her theology.

We create this book as educators, influenced – as so many others – by her life and vision. Rather than create a book of reminiscences, of tributes to her achievements, we – together with the other contributors – wished this book to be a celebration of her life, a mouthpiece for all those who, unnoticed and unsung, numbed by the sadness of her going, yet remain faithful to her vision. We create this book as no mere replica of her achievements – indeed, there are many gaps – nor as a comprehensive compendium of sacramentology. What seemed to us the greatest tribute to Christiane, what she would have wished, is to carry the torch further. *Keep the candles burning.*

Our context has changed – in Europe the Wall is down and we live in a post-communist era. In the United States, President Clinton struggles with the tides of refugees from Cuba and Haiti, and in Africa the world witnesses the agony of Rwanda. As we write, the World Council of Churches has declared a Decade in Solidarity with Women and the Roman Catholic Church is in the midst of a Decade of Evangelization; 1994 has been the Year of the Family. Our theology responds to all these contexts. We also wish to develop a theology of the sacraments which is ecumenical in character – and eventually we hope that this will acquire an inter-faith dimension. And, finally, we want to develop strands of sacramental theology which show how the work of Christiane has borne fruit, and continues to blossom further, in ways which she could not have imagined.

Thus we have grouped articles which illustrate these different aspects. Part One concentrates more on theological dimensions. In the first two articles Mary Grey and Anne Kelly develop key insights from feminist sacramental spirituality, stressing mutuality in relating, inclusivity, ecological grace and prophetic grieving. This is paralleled by Enda McDonagh's reflection on ecological and justice aspects of the Eucharist, John Sutcliffe's thoughts on 'the Eucharist and learning' from a United Reformed Church perspective, and a profound meditation on 'Reconciliation' by Patrick Purnell. Three historical chapters look at the historical roots of catechesis (Damian Lundy), the richness of mystagogical catechesis (Catherine Dooley), and, rooted in tradition and in church documents, a reflection on a spirituality for ordained priests (Kenan Osborne). This section ends with a theological reflection by Susan Roll on 'Time in the sacraments and the liturgical year' and a meditation by Andrée Heaton on 'Waiting' as a leitmotiv for a sacramental spirituality.

Part Two is faithful to 'sharing our story' and 'the sacramental journey' in its different settings. Mary Bernard Potter reflects on renewal from the two contexts of her religious congregation and the parish community, and Angela Lawrence from a diocesan perspective. The two following chapters focus directly on Christiane's deepest concern: children and young people. (Her last work was a Lectionary for children.) Thus Danny Sullivan writes of the spirituality of children, and Julia Houlston and Perry Gildea present a vision of a chaplaincy experience with students. John Logan's contribution – written from a Methodist perspective – attempts to expand the focus on sacrament as exclusively Christian, by introducing an inter-faith perspective. We end with a reflection on prophecy and suffering which invites all who have contributed or wished to contribute to this book, those who worked with Christiane Brusselmans, and all who were influenced by her life and work, to remember her in the context of the prophet's willingness to suffer, in order that the world may be brought to the justice, peace and unquenchable hope of God's Kingdom.

Mary Grey, Andrée Heaton, Danny Sullivan

September 1994

Part One

Part One

Beyond exclusion

towards a feminist eucharistic ecclesiology

MARY GREY

If THERE WAS ONE ISSUE which Christiane Brusselmans stood for consistently, it was that mothers were the rightful educators of their children, especially in passing on the light of faith. Though never a self-confessed feminist, more than anyone I know she affirmed women as religious educators and theologians. In my own case, she stood by me, encouraging me forward from the first class (her own) in 1973, until my inaugural lecture as Professor of Feminism and Christianity at the Catholic University of Nijmegen in 1989. Sacramental experience was the heart of her theology: and it was her conviction that sacraments are rooted in human living which inspires me to take further what I tried to do in 1983, in *In Search of the Sacred*:[1] namely, exploring the sacraments from human experience, but this time bringing feminist insights to bear on these reflections.

But this chapter is written when feminist theologians in the Roman Catholic Church are heavy-hearted, in the wake of the Apostolic Letter from the Vatican (May 1994), stating firmly that the Church does not have the authority to ordain women. It comes as a particularly harsh blow for women, when so many of us have supported the struggle of the women in the Church of England, and shared the euphoria of the ordinations of more than a thousand women priests, from April to July 1994.[2] But instead of regarding this as the end of the road, I will take it as a challenge to deepen the very notion of sacrament. What I attempt in this chapter is to outline some key notions of sacrament, incorporating insights from feminist theology and Women's Studies. I will try to show that these insights are actually pointing to something profound about the meaning of *Church*. My

3

method is to take selected themes of Christiane Brusselmans' eucharistic programme as jumping-off points for reflection.[3]

BELONGING – AND RE-ENVISIONING THE SACRAMENTAL COMMUNITY

Sacraments – as Karl Rahner and Edward Schillebeeckx have taught us[4] – are both encounters with the presence of Christ and constitutive of being Christian Church. Sacraments touch women at the most vulnerable core of their being. For, despite the pain of exclusion from the ordained ministry, which effectively means denying the sacramental ministry of women and lay men – Matrimony being the only exception to this, and Baptism, in exceptional circumstances – there is a love and a loyalty to the Church which defies explanation. It is a loyalty and an obstinate belief that the Church – despite its patriarchal ordering, the corrupt periods of its history, and its refusal to hear the voices of the liberation theologians – is nonetheless the Community of the Beloved One. Despite all the injustices and the disempowering of lay people, it is the belief that the Church is still proclaiming the vision of the Kingdom of God.

It is with this conviction that the Women-Church movement was born. Not that women wish to found another Church of Christ or even another organization. But, growing out of the reforms of Vatican II, in the flowering of the baptismal ministry of being called to minister, has sprung a global movement, Women-Church, to call attention to the fact that *women are church*, are the pilgrim people of God, and to call women out of the shadows of Christian tradition to their full sacramental vocation.[5] Rosemary Ruether has called this an exodus movement, an exodus from patriarchy which is seen as wrong or *alienated relationship*:

> As Women-Church we claim the authentic mission of Christ, the true mission of the Church, the real agenda of our Mother-Father God who comes to restore and not destroy our humanity, who comes to ransom the captives and reclaim the earth as our Promised land.[6]

Some feel that the description of Women-Church as exodus community does not do justice to women's deep desire to belong, and to create community. It does not do justice to the fact that despite exclusion from structures, it is women who have educated their children in faith, and who have worked to build the sacramental community from the earliest days of Christianity. The beautiful medieval iconography of the trinity of St Anne, Mary and Jesus illustrates this. Anne is shown as teaching Mary, who is teaching Jesus. This was the tradition on which Luther was building when he wrote his great Catechism. This was the tradition which Christiane Brusselmans was reclaiming with 'Les mamans catéchistes'.

A more inspiring image for Women-Church is 'the discipleship of equals', the idea of Christian community as promoting the full becoming of women and men in a juster, more inclusive manner of relating. The idea was first expressed by Elisabeth Schüssler-Fiorenza and developed in many of her works.[7] In my own work I develop the idea of Christian community as healing space, as redeeming community, where redemption means the mutuality of giving and receiving the energy and power of healing, the power to make right relation, embodied in Christ.[8] Sacrament is experienced in the concretizing of right relation, in the development of a spirituality of relatedness. For this sacramental spirituality the notion of celebration is vital.

Celebrating sacred time, sacred space

A feminist spirituality of redemption attempts to transcend the dualisms constricting sacramental theology, specifically the boundary between the sacred and the profane. Too many precious areas of human experience never reach articulation as sacramental because of this undervaluing of anything associated with the physical and sexual. I recall my own shock after giving birth to children, experiences which I found both exhilarating and creative, pulling me into wonderment at the creative energies of God, to realize that this experience was in no way reflected in the baptismal liturgy, which rather focused – inappropriately, I felt – on the baby's renunciation of sin.

But the experiences of nursing, feeding, the eucharistic moments of sharing meals (not only with children, but with friends, students, lovers), the coffee we drink at political protest meetings, the rituals we create spontaneously to celebrate the seasons, or the passing of milestones in life: all are expressions of our communities of redemptive mutuality.

There is a deeper meaning to celebration which is found among the poorest women of the world, communities which are doubly oppressed, from within and without. *Struggle to Be the Sun Again* is the title of the Korean theologian Chung Hyun Kyung's book: she summons poor Korean women to shine once more with their own strength and energy, expressing the vitality and courage which many communities of women show even in the midst of intense suffering.[9] In the midst of these stories of suffering and violence a new meaning is given to Christian discipleship: one that does not accept or condone suffering, but that resists and protests. This is giving rise to a theology of the Cross that does not idealize crucifixions.[10] It is a theology of the Cross which does not take away suffering, but gives us *a way of seeing in the dark*.

Making peace – commitment to a process

Such a theology of the Cross opens up a new dimension for sacramental reconciliation. Here women often experience a double-bind. 'Keep the peace', 'Don't rock the boat' is advice frequently given to women in family situations, even in cases of domestic violence. It is to women that people look to make initiatives of peace, to represent the binding function which draws communities together. The way forward I suggest is in two steps. An icon of sacramental peace-making was offered by the Women's Peace Camps at Greenham Common. It was a movement of *protest* and *resistance* – the first step – against the presence of Cruise Missiles in Britain, yet it was enacted in terms of *building an alternative community*, using images of peace and joy, because the world was being envisioned differently. This is the second step. It is no accident that movements of reconciliation originate from the victims of violence – we are seeing the same phenomenon in the building of a post-apartheid South Africa. Thus the ministry of Reconciliation draws on Paul's words, 'In Christ, we are a new creation' (2 Corinthians 5): but the new creation stems from a commitment to peace with justice. As Marie Fortune, Director of the Centre for Domestic Violence, says: forgiveness is a process; at the deepest level it is an act of mutuality.[11] Where the mutuality is absent, commitment to the process of healing is essential. And this involves obtaining as much reparation as is possible. For example, it may be impossible for a raped woman to obtain repentance from the rapist: but it is possible for her to be helped towards regaining self-esteem, to be helped financially, for her to experience liturgies of healing. For this we need a new theology of sacramental proclamation.

PROCLAIMING THE WORD AND THE
MINISTRY OF LISTENING

Women's spirituality – like many base communities devoted to justice and peace – grows and is nurtured by the experience of 'telling our stories'. But in this case the stories of the voiceless – women silenced by experiences of suffering, or prevented from speech by not being theologically literate, or not authorized to preach – are being 'heard into speech'.[12] Hence much of the activity of Women-Church – as communities of redemptive mutuality – focuses on providing this healing space where the stories can be told. This is the first challenge posed to the official ecclesial sacramental liturgy: give voice to the unheard stories of suffering – violence against women, discrimination against ethnic minorities, vilification of gay people, ostracism of AIDS sufferers. Let the links be made between the healing of the brokenhearted people of the Christian gospels and those today. This is the word which needs to be proclaimed, in the face of the Pharaohs of individualism, greed and competition.

Second, the word which is proclaimed must be inclusive of all human and non-human experience. The mystery of God embodied today is too profound to be restricted to images, metaphors and symbols of one sex only. Redemptive communities need to express their vulnerability, their longings and desires, and to know these as rooted in the fathomless being of God. Calling on God as our mother, our lover and our friend, opens up the floodgates of a revitalized religious experience which values the physical, emotional side of human nature. Calling on God as light, running water, dove, eagle, roaring wind, awakens us to the presence of God in nature, recalling the mystical, contemplative tradition, largely ignored in a culture where the soundbite reigns supreme.[13] In fact, the liturgical recognition of ignored dimensions of humanity may even evoke the rediscovery of the Father symbol, at a time when human fatherhood is at risk (witness the number of cases of child abuse), a crisis partly caused by the prevalence of distorted images of masculinity.

Third, ministry as listening, to the stories, to the signs of the times, must be part of the recovery of ministering in mutuality, part of the response to the narratives of suffering. Christ as Logos, the Word made flesh, is not the one-sided Word proclaimed by the powerful to passive listeners; rather, Christ as Logos *restores mutuality to the word*, enables communication where the dynamic is one of making right relation. As Carter Heyward wrote:

We are driven back to speak the Word that spills among us: 'Without our touching, there is no God. Without our crying, our yearning, our raging, there is no God. For in the beginning is the relation, and in the relation is the power that creates the world, through us, and with us, and by us, you and I, you and we, and none of us alone.'[14]

This is the sacramental meaning of breaking the word together: that in our commitment, our passion for justice-making, the Christic healing and transformative power-in-relation is given new embodiment. This new embodiment is rooted in the new psychology of care issuing from Women's Studies.[15]

CARING, *DIAKONIA* AND FEMINISM

Diakonia has always been at the heart of sacramental life, originating in the responsibility of caring for the poor, sick, orphaned and strangers in the earliest Christian community (Acts 4:34–35, 6:1–6). It is a ministry rooted also in Judaism (see, for example, Deuteronomy 24:17). Women have a remarkable history in the *diakonia* of the Church. Numerous saints have led the way in caring for the destitute – from Elizabeth of Hungary to the foundresses of religious congregations in the wake of the French Revolution. But, like the double-bind which surrounds women in the area of peace-making, 'caring' is also an ambiguous area. As described in the recent best-seller *Women Who Love Too Much*,[16] the problem for many women is both that they care too much, and that essentialist determinations of female human nature have repeatedly decreed that women's role is to care, preferably as mothers – biological or spiritual – putting much emphasis on the pseudo-Pauline text of 1 Timothy 2:16, 'Yet women shall be saved by bearing children'.[17]

But we now understand both that caring is so important that it should not become the property of one sex alone, and that some women have difficulty in reaching a sense of selfhood at all, so effective is their socialization. They are inclined to lose self, to sacrifice their own becoming to the vocation to care, be it on the one hand for ageing parents, husband or children, or on the other hand, in some suitable work – nursing or social work. A feminist theology of care stresses, first, the mutuality of the caring process – the carer, too, has needs. (We have begun to recognize this, as, sadly, carers of elderly senile parents often die before those whom they are looking after.) Every human person is called to full personhood, not in the Western over-individualized call to self-indulgence, but in the call to grow into full capacity to become a person-in-relation. Second, that caring is not merely at a personal level, but must grapple with the structures of caring, with the Health and Social Services systems, the care available for the misfits and marginalized. It is the task of the sacramental community to ensure that the much maligned phrase 'care in the community' actually makes the links between liturgy and the structures of injustice on a global level. And there is a further level of caring: care for creation.

CARING FOR CREATION, THANKING FOR CREATION

A eucharistic ecclesiology is also rooted in an organic theology of creation. In the conviction that the risen Jesus drew the whole of creation – soil, trees, birds, animals, galaxies – into the process of becoming the Kingdom of God, the liturgy is celebrated. In the conviction that the earthly Jesus learnt from, appreciated and worked with the humblest aspects of nature – mustard seed, blood, grass, weeds, salt, oil and water – sacramental experience refuses to spiritualize the *grounded nature of ecological grace*. From ecofeminist insights, which coincide with some of Christianity's oldest but understressed intuitions, springs the conviction that redemption and salvation for humanity cannot be enacted and brought to fulfilment without the fulfilment and healing of the universe itself. The two must go together. 'The entire creation has been groaning in one great act of giving birth', wrote Paul (Romans 8); and as Tillich said in one of his sermons, 'Nature, too, mourns for a lost good . . .'[18] Liturgy should enable us to recover that lost sense of connection with nature, in all its glory and terror, our indebtedness to the earth, our listening to nature as Teacher, and our joint responsibility for eco-justice. As Adrienne Rich put it: a vanished pride and care still urge us on, 'to help the earth deliver'.[19] Such a task is what redemption as right relatedness means. It means re-imaging atonement not as victory over death (with overtones of glorification of warfare), not as a ransom price demanded by the wounded honour of God (too much tainted with medieval lawcourt symbolism), and not as a call to be crucified with Jesus (which sometimes leads to an idealization of suffering). The eucharistic theme which Christiane Brusselmans called 'Thanks for new life' means exactly that: that the life which sprang from the Cross event – the murder of an innocent man – is the atonement seen as *birth-*

giving, creating new and just forms of life, by rejecting all that is necrophilic or death-dealing, and embodying right relation in history. Thus, far from rejecting atonement, we liberate the whole process of Christ's reconciliation from association with a wrathful God, with a God who sent an innocent child to death – what Rita Brock calls 'divine child abuse'[20] – reclaiming sacrifice, not as the death of a rightful sense of self, but as a voluntary living out of ideals in the service of the Kingdom of God.

SHARING A MEAL AND BECOMING ICONS OF CHRIST

Many Christians experienced the eucharistic presidency of women for the first time following the Church of England ordinations in 1994. For the first time their intuitions were confirmed: that it was the most natural thing in the world for the hands that have prepared, served and cleared away meals for centuries to preside at the table of the Lord's supper. It is still my hope that the liturgical experiencing of women's presidency may so lift our awareness of what it means to be 'icons of Christ' (the priest acting *in persona Christi*), as to bring us out of the current impasse which threatens ecumenical relationships.

It is my hope that women's presidency will be a non-hierarchical one; that the inclusivity which characterizes the language and praxis of women's spirituality may make us conscious of the priestly nature of all Christian life, of the sacred character of our eating together, of the holiness of the physical and sexual. Women's spirituality begins with the concrete, the embodied and the particular, not in order to spiritualize their significance, but to see this earthiness as blessed. Second, my hope is that this very inclusiveness will make the connections between the bread that is blessed, the wine that is poured, and the hunger, the failure of the crops, the desertified soil, the polluted water – which are the realities for many parts of the body of Christ. In other words, that the liturgical will never be separated from social and political realities. Third, my hope is that becoming icons of Christ, women eucharistic presidents may become an inclusive image of ministry for the whole body of Christ, eliminating the distance between priest and people, drawing us out of a privatized notion of community: it is as a community that we stand before God, and we have been schooled in separation and individualist responses. If women's ministry can break open our consciousness into communal thinking and action, then we will truly be sharing a meal, the Lord's supper.

★

Finally, Christiane Brusselmans ends with the great hope of 'Going forth to make a better world'. Just as the apostles at Emmaus, after their hearts burned within them at the table-sharing with Jesus, ran back to Jerusalem to spread the good news; so must eucharistic liturgy flow into life and back again. What I believe a feminist eucharistic ecclesiology to be is working towards a new experience of prophetic community. Prophecy, not as the utterings of one individual but of a prophetic community, where a shared vision of mutuality and right relation empowers its members to make incarnate their shared vision of redeemed reality. Transcending the dualisms of being and doing, body and spirit brings about on the one hand an experience of prayer as energy, as the energy to enter into deeper relation; on the other hand a vitality in the discovery of painting, poems, dance – of embodied prayer forms. Above all, the ability to gather the fragments – of brokenness, of alienated dualisms, of warped experience of community, of burnt-out people – this is the seal of a redemptive sacramental community, where baptismal anointing takes on new meaning. Broken people, long voiceless, are anointed into speech, into a ministry of caring and being cared-for. And this, as Christiane would say, can only be the work of the Holy Spirit, the special giftedness coming into fruition, to some extent at least, because of the seeds which she sowed.

NOTES

1. Mary Grey, *In Search of the Sacred: Sacraments and Parish Renewal* (Wheathampstead: Anthony Clarke Books, 1983).
2. In my own case, after preaching at Lichfield Cathedral on 22 and 23 April, at the ordination of 51 women priests, the Apostolic Letter came as a particular shock. The sense of elation and enormous hope that at last some of the wounds of history could be healed, the expectation that the Church could now experience a different kind of ministry, were removed at one fell swoop.
3. Christiane Brusselmans, *We Celebrate the Eucharist* (Morristown, NJ: Silver Burdett, 1971). The nine themes are: It's about belonging; Celebrating; Making peace; Listening; Caring; Giving thanks for creation; Giving thanks for new life; Sharing a meal; and Going forth to make a better world.
4. See for example Edward Schillebeeckx, *Christ the Sacrament of the Encounter with God* (New York: Sheed and Ward, 1963); Karl Rahner, 'Jesus Christ' in *Foundations of Religious Faith* (London: Darton, Longman and Todd, 1978), pp. 178–321.
5. For the history of the Women-Church movement, see Mary-Jo Weaver, *New Catholic Women: A Contemporary Challenge to Traditional Religious Authority* (San Francisco:

Harper and Row, 1985); Rosemary Ruether, *Women-Church: Theology and Practice* (New York: Harper and Row, 1985); Elisabeth Schüssler-Fiorenza, *In Memory of Her* (London: SCM Press, 1980) and *Bread Not Stone: The Challenge of Feminist Biblical Scholarship* (Boston: Beacon Press, 1984); Mary Grey, *The Wisdom of Fools?* (London: SPCK, 1993), ch. 9.

6. Ruether, op. cit., p. 72.

7. As well as *In Memory of Her* and *Bread Not Stone*, already cited, see *Discipleship of Equals: An Ecclesialogy of Liberation* (New York: Crossroad, 1993), which is a compilation of Schüssler-Fiorenza's most significant writings on Women-Church.

8. Mary Grey, *Redeeming the Dream* (London: SPCK, 1989).

9. Chung Hyun Kyung, *Struggle to Be the Sun Again* (Maryknoll, NY: Orbis, 1991).

10. See Beverly Harrison, 'The power of anger and the work of love' in Carol Robb (ed.), *Making the Connections* (Boston: Beacon Press, 1986).

11. See Marie Fortune, *Sexual Violence: The Unmentionable Sin* (New York: Pilgrim, 1983) and *Is Nothing Sacred?: When Sex Invades the Pastoral Relationship* (San Francisco: Harper and Row, 1989).

12. The phrase 'being heard into speech' originates from the late Nelle Morton, *The Journey Is Home* (Boston: Beacon Press, 1986).

13. See Sallie McFague, *The Body of God* (London: SCM Press, 1993); Janet Morley, *All Desires Known* (London: Movement for the Ordination of Women/Women In Theology, 1988).

14. Carter Heyward, *The Redemption of God* (Washington, DC: University of America Press, 1982).

15. See especially Carol Gilligan, *In a Different Voice?* (Cambridge, MA: Harvard University Press, 1982); Jean Baker Miller, *Towards a New Psychology of Women* (Boston: Beacon Press, 1976).

16. Robin Norwood, *Women Who Love Too Much* (London: Arrow Books, 1986).

17. See Mary Grey, 'Yet women shall be saved by bearing children: motherhood and the possibility of contemporary discourse for women', *Bijdragen: Tijdschrift voor Filosofie en Theologie* 52 (1991), pp. 58–69.

18. Paul Tillich, 'Nature mourns for a lost good' in *The Shaking of the Foundations* (Harmondsworth: Penguin, 1963), pp. 82–92.

19. Adrienne Rich, 'Natural Resources' in *The Dream of a Common Language* (New York: W.W. Norton, 1978), pp. 65–6.

20. Rita Brock, 'And a little child shall lead us' in Rebecca Parker and Carol S. Bohn (eds), *God So Loved the World: Christianity, Patriarchy and Abuse* (New York: Pilgrim, 1989).

To 'reconstitute the world'

the sacramental imagination and a spirituality of embodiment

ANNE F. KELLY

> My heart is moved by all I cannot save
> so much has been destroyed
> I have to cast my lot with those
> who age after age, perversely,
> with no extraordinary power,
> reconstitute the world.[1]

'THINKING POETICALLY, acting poetically or dwelling poetically are all modalities of imagining poetically. They are all ways of realizing the *possibilities* of what we are. As the poet Emily Dickinson wrote ... "possibility is the fuse lit by the spark of imagination." '[2] Within the Christian tradition, sacramental celebrations can be interpreted as the poetic texts that have enabled Christians to imagine newness and possibility, by proposing to the imagination new ways of being in the world.[3] If they are to continue to do so, our hermeneutics of suspicion must ask some serious questions. Can the traditional ways of thinking about and celebrating sacraments include difference, particularity and bodiliness that moves beyond dualistic categories? Can they represent other than patterns of domination? Can they accommodate liberating praxis? Can they enable us to grieve? These questions are the lenses through which I seek to imagine sacramentally an alternative vision of reality faithful to feminist and liberation hermeneutics. To explore how the sacramental imagination can indeed offer a poetics of the possible I intend to look at four different though interrelated areas:

(1) prophetic grieving,
(2) telling a new story,
(3) ecstatically experiencing new connections, and
(4) transformative praxis.

Such imagining should be taking place within committed communities, whether they are marginalized communities of celebration and resistance[4] or more traditional communities of word and sacrament.

(1) PROPHETIC GRIEVING

Compassionate grieving is the first step – confronting the psychic numbness, overcoming the paralysis of imagination, beginning to imagine newness, life in the place of death, remembering in the place of forgetting. It is time to resurrect the body.[5] The body as the place where we encounter God. The body of the world in all its brokenness and woundedness. The broken bodies of the suffering, the bruised body of the earth itself, the battered and abused bodies broken by relationships and systems of injustice. Restoring bodiliness as integral to the story of who we are must begin with this lamenting and grieving. For we must grieve our lost connections, our disembodied knowing and our disengaged spiritualities. And primarily it is the bodies of women we must re-member. For at the heart of patriarchal imagining is fear, mistrust, denial and at times loathing of the female body. The dualistic thinking that elevates mind, man, spirit and God and which in turn degrades body, female, nature and earth can only give rise to fractured memory and impoverished imaginations.

The task of the prophet is sometimes to grieve that things are not as they should be. It is as if only grieving can begin to open the space where we might imagine newness. The retrieval of bodiliness as integral to spirituality must begin with a ritual lament for the bodies of women. Irish poet Anne Le Marquand Hartigan's choral poem 'La Corbiére' tells the story of the drowning of many women prostitutes after a shipwreck during World War II.

> In clusters your bodies dance,
> together you're flowers, yellow
> hair spread on the sea's time.[6]

The poignancy of her lament is deepened by the repetition of the line 'No one is coming'. The poem itself in its language, grieving and lamentation becomes the ritual and the holy burial these women's lives need.

> I will weep for thee
> mourn for thee
> cry for thee
> in the strong salt sea will long for thee
> sing for thee
> sea sister water sister
> we will howl for thee.[7]

Their bodies have been used, abused, and now lie discarded on the 'indifferent sea'.[8] Can these bodies truly be the bodies of Christ? Women's bodies so often the spoils of war. Women's bodies all too often victimized within the crushing hierarchies of patriarchal dualistic thinking.

'There is no answer but stone.'[9] The ageless story that calls to mind other stories: Lot's wife, Hagar's abandonment, Rachel's weeping, Tamar's rape, Jephthah's daughter sacrificed as her father's vow demanded, the Levite's concubine, her body abused and mutilated. Such texts of terror that demand a cry, a howl from the body's pain. Such re-membering of our sister's pain, our own pain, leaves us keening in the ancient way of the *bean caointe*[10] in the Irish tradition. It is not simply enough to say we know the story. All need to feel the pain in and through their bodies. The pain of remembering, the refusal to be reconciled,[11] involves holding on to the grief until we have wept all tears, until we have told all the stories, until we have created the rituals that will re-member them. Through the pain of re-membering, through the salt tears of the weeping will we begin to re-member ourselves and our world?

(2) TELLING A NEW STORY

It is time to consider again the stories and myths by which we live. To know the stories that ground us. If we are to be a people who can reconstitute the world, we need to be thinking and imagining differently. We need new root metaphors, new paradigms, new dreaming to inspire new action. To live within any myth in the postmodern age is complex. It is to know we are dreaming but to keep dreaming.[12] It is to include the dangerous memories of suffering that Metz speaks about; it is to include the narratives of the lost and forgotten. And in our time it is to include the story of the earth itself. Whether a new metaphor like that of connected-ness can enable us to imagine a new set of relationships with ourselves, our bodies, society and the earth remains to be seen. Can the traditional story of Incarnation be expanded to include bodiliness in ways not yet imagined?

Can the convenantal and sacramental traditions provide the kind of uniting of the ethical and aesthetic imagination that enables one both to be faithful to the Judaeo-Christian tradition and also to embrace aspects of the Gaia tradition? If genuine anamnesis and an analogical imagination[13] are the way to imagine a future while remaining faithful to the past vision, then such remembering will have to become genuinely metanoic.[14] A metanoia that involves the grieving I have already spoken about but also one that can genuinely turn to the other and embrace it: whether the other is female, the body, cycles of life and decay, the shadow, the dark, whatever is different, whatever it is that we fear, even death itself. Without this embrace, fear of and demonizing of the other takes place. A memory and imagination that cannot engage in this metanoia will be sterile and powerless.

In telling a new story we are hoping to nurture a biophilic conscious-ness.[15] Such a love of life and all its processes demands a conversion of the imagination to this new way of seeing. It is a radical reversal of the familiar patterns of domination that are death-dealing to their core. It is a vision of reality as graced to the core. It is an invitation to find that the ordinary is extraordinary. It is a way of uniting immanence and transcendence. The way to know God is intimately through the integrity of all creation. It is to nurture a spirituality that allows 'epiphanies of connection' even in the midst of brokenness.[16] The embrace of particularity and difference demands that our experiences of God 'bless the ordinary' and 'sanctify the common'.[17]

(3) ECSTATICALLY EXPERIENCING NEW CONNECTIONS

Ruether believes that a healed relationship with each other, the earth and the divine calls for a new symbolic culture and spirituality.[18] Ruether's attempts to engage in this new imagining involve embracing both the convenantal and sacramental traditions, which she sees as complementary, rather than alternatives. 'The one tradition shapes our relation to nature and each other in terms of law and ethical responsibility. The other tradition ecstatically experiences the divine bodying forth into the cosmos, and beckons us into communion.'[19]

Such an entering into communion is evoked most beautifully in Brian Keenan's book *An Evil Cradling*. One morning Keenan returns as usual to his filthy cell. He is expecting nothing more than its familiar monotonous greyness when he sees a brown bowl of fruits, apricots, oranges, nuts, cherries, a banana.

> The fruits, the colours mesmerize me in a quiet rapture that spins through my head. I am entranced by colour. I lift an orange into the flat filthy palm of my hand and feel and smell and lick it. The colour orange, the colour, the colour, my God the colour orange. Before me is a feast of colour. I feel myself begin to dance slowly . . .
>
> I cannot, I will not eat this fruit. I sit in joy, so complete, beyond the meaning of joy. My soul finds its own completeness in that bowl of colour. The forms of each fruit. The shape and curl and bend all so rich, so perfect. I want to bow before it, loving that blazing, roaring, orange colour . . . Everything meeting in a moment of colour and of form, my rapture no longer an abstract euphoria. It is there in that tiny bowl, the world recreated in that broken bowl. I feel the smell of each fruit leaping into me and lifting me and carrying me away. I am drunk with something that I understand but cannot explain. I am filled with a sense of love. I am filled and satiated by it. What I have waited and longed for has without my knowing come to me, and taken all of me.[20]

His rapture, his amazement, his joy and his ability to enter into the world created by the fruit reminds me of Paul Ricoeur's interpretation of revelation as the calling into the heart of existence of the imagination of the possible. The fruit which Keenan could not eat became a symbol of the possible, a way of imagining, dreaming another world, a new way of being.

If we engage in befriending our symbols, in letting the symbols speak, in allowing them to interpret us, perhaps they will disclose a new way of being in the world. New symbols and metaphors emerge from transformed consciousness in a way that can enable us to see the old in a new way. Where the metaphors have collapsed into identity, new metaphors and ways of imagining can break open the closed ways of seeing and disclose new worlds. If we are to truly experience our interrelationship and kinship with all living things in this great web of life, 'a profound spirituality would arise'.[21] Such an ethic and spirituality might be capable of 'calling us to the tasks of healing and sustaining the earth'.[22] Finding a language for these new experiences means calling in the poets, the artists, the dreamers. The aesthetic imagination must be nurtured so that we can learn how to deeply experience and how to deeply imagine a future.

(4) TRANSFORMATIVE PRAXIS

The task for the ethical imagination arising out of an embodied spirituality is simply to reconstitute the world.

> The problem is
> to connect, without hysteria, the pain
> of any one's body with the pain of the body's world
> For it is the body's world
> they are trying to destroy forever.[23]

The compassionate grieving and reweaving of the web of life begins with an experience of such brokenness that one is almost rendered powerless in the face of it. The collapse of symbol systems under the weight of our hermeneutics of suspicion can leave us feeling rootless and lost in our dreaming. And yet we must go on. I was very struck with the passage in Jeanette Winterson's *Sexing the Cherry*[24] where, in a country church, the fragments of a stained-glass window depicting the feeding of the five thousand, shattered by cannon during the Civil War, are lovingly collected into baskets by local women. Even where the beautiful window has been destroyed the women's careful work of restoration, in solidarity and in love, becomes the living symbol of what cannot ever be destroyed.

Christians have always held strongly to the bodily resurrection of Jesus. The broken bruised body that experiences death is the one that is transformed. Bodiliness is integral to the resurrection story. The disciples eat bread and fish with this risen Jesus. They are invited to touch his hands and feet, to know he lives.

Hearts are moved when we yearn for restoration of relationships, when we grieve that things are not as they should be, when we dare to imagine newness and possibility. We must weep with Rachel before we can laugh with Sarah. A compassionate commitment to transformation is our daily witness to the bodily resurrection of Jesus. It requires no extraordinary power.

IMAGINING THE FUTURE

The Christian community has long been a people of memory and imagination. Our remembering and dreaming have long gone hand in hand. Imagining the present from the perspective of the future, while remaining faithful to anamnesis, is one of the principal expressions of the eucharistic community. If we are to imagine abundance of life for all creation we must begin by restoring the body to its central place in spirituality. The body must be interruptive of our imagining. This will enable us to move beyond dualistic patterns of thought which separate body and soul, male and female, heaven and earth, thought and action. The uniting of the aesthetic and ethical imagination pivots on this restoration of the body as central to our imagining. We have not yet found a language to express these new connections. We have only analogy, symbol, metaphor, myth. Such a language that speaks the body, that speaks connection rather than separation, has not yet been heard. Perhaps when this speaking begins we will develop a new poetics based on creativity and poetic language. Until then, as Emily Dickinson says, we can only 'tell it slant'. I conclude my musings with a poem I wrote for my daughter on her eighth birthday.

EARTHBALL

Little one this is your day
hush let me whisper how I love you.
how your eyes are glowing
now beside us in our bed.
eight years now since first we lay together
separate but at one
sharing the exhaustion
of your birthing.

No tiredness now
you've been awake for hours
your bedroom strewn with cards and wrappings
your excitement wakens the child in me

and I hear you speak in wonder
of how you love the Earthball
we have given you.

Someday you will learn
that we call that ball a globe
and no longer use your word
in case they laugh.
my gift to you is memory
lest you forget this naming
and the hope
that in remembering
you may shape a new imagining
for this Earthball world of ours.

NOTES

1. Adrienne Rich, 'Natural Resources' in *The Dream of a Common Language* (New York: Norton, 1978), p. 67.
2. Richard Kearney, *Poetics of Imagining* (London: HarperCollins, 1991), p. 162. Emphasis in original.
3. Cf. my own article on this topic, 'Disclosing the passion for the possible: interpreting sacraments as life's interpreters' in Dermot A. Lane (ed.), *Religion and Culture in Dialogue* (Dublin: Columba Press, 1993), pp. 64–84.
4. R. R. Ruether, *Gaia and God* (London: SCM Press, 1993), pp. 268–74.
5. Naomi R. Goldenberg believes that 'Since Western Religious thought cannot reveal the physical and social contingency of human life, we must turn to other ways of thinking, such as psychoanalysis and feminism, to resurrect the body': 'Apocalypse in everyday life: the cultural context in which we do theory' in *Resurrecting The Body: Feminism, Religion and Psychoanalysis* (New York: Crossroad, 1993), p. 6. Later in the book (p. 40) she refers to the work of feminist philosophers whose work she sees as a writing that resurrects the body.
6. Anne Le Marquand Hartigan, 'La Corbiére' in *Immortal Sins* (Dublin: Salmon, 1993), p. 148.
7. Ibid., p. 141.
8. Ibid., p. 149.
9. Ibid., p. 144.
10. The *caoineadh* is an ancient form of lament from the Celtic tradition. Women ritually wept (or keened) for the dead in haunting music, with words and repeated refrains like 'Och, Ochón', which told the story of the dead person and lamented their passing. Great displays of grief, including tearing out one's hair and weeping loudly and uncontrollably, often accompanied these. Women were eventually forbidden by the Church authorities to engage in such public demonstrations of grief.

11. Karen Gershon writes in her poetry about the refusal to be reconciled to the past – a past that involves her heritage as a Jewish woman who never saw her parents again after she was sent to England during World War II. Cf. Karen Gershon, 'Monologue' in *Collected Poems* (London: Papermac, 1990), p. 33.

12. Kearney, op. cit., p. 183.

13. Writing on the role of imagination in the postmodern era, Kearney states 'Post-modernity designates an attitude governed by the prefix *ana-* – *anamnesis* (to re-collect and re-create what has been eclipsed by history) or *analogy* (to say one thing in terms of another)': ibid., p. 215. Emphasis in original.

14. Mary Grey writes about 'a "metanoic" memory, a remembering which fearlessly and with humility "makes the connections". And the connections bring about metanoia or conversion': *The Wisdom of Fools?* (London: SPCK, 1993), p. 116.

15. R. R. Ruether writes 'Life is sustained by biotic relationality, in which the whole attains a plenitude through mutual limits in interdependency ... Only by eschewing paranoid projection of all evil onto malignant "aliens" can we begin to reconstruct the tissues of relationship in a way that produces more biotic plenitude and less toxic violence': op. cit., pp. 141, 142.

16. Grey, op. cit., p. 61.

17. Eavan Boland, 'Envoi' in *Selected Poems* (Manchester: Carcanet, 1989), p. 90.

18. Ruether, op. cit., p. 4.

19. Ibid., p. 9.

20. Brian Keenan, *An Evil Cradling* (London: Hutchinson, 1992), pp. 68–9.

21. Ruether, op. cit., p. 48.

22. Ibid., p. 58.

23. Adrienne Rich, 'Contradictions: Tracking Poems' in *Your Native Land, Your Life* (New York: Norton, 1986), p. 100.

24. Jeanette Winterson, *Sexing the Cherry* (London: Vintage, 1990), pp. 63–4.

Fruit of the earth – work of human hands

a prophetic theology of the Eucharist

ENDA MCDONAGH

IN THE RENEWAL of sacramental life and understanding, to which Christiane Brusselmans made such a remarkable contribution, Catholic centrality of the Eucharist has appeared to survive intact. In the words of Augustine Birrell from his days as First Secretary in Ireland, 'It is still the Mass that matters'. It certainly matters in official exhortation and theological reflection as it matters to millions of ordinary Sunday and daily mass-goers. The millions of Catholics who never or rarely attend Mass either through choice or necessity must qualify the easy assumption of centrality. Where their lack of attendance is necessitated by shortage of male celibate priests, the official emphasis on the centrality of the Eucharist must also be qualified. A particular model of ordained priesthood may be treated as more important in practice than providing the priestly people with the opportunity to celebrate Eucharist.

The Eucharist as centre of the Church's sacraments (Aquinas *et al.*) and of the Church as sacrament (Rahner, Schillebeeckx *et al.*) has dominated much of the Catholic theological discussion. The ecumenical discussion has sought to integrate these insights with the concerns of the Reformed and Orthodox Churches in a variety of ways. The parameters of these discussions within and between churches have been ecclesial and salvific. Redemption and salvation, sacrifice and meal, presence and symbol, have been the currency of what has been really an in-house debate of the *domus Dei (Jesu Christi)*. In an increasingly post-Christian and, however one interprets it exactly, postmodern context, such debate may appear marginal, eccentric rather than central. In a world threatened by human destructiveness militarily and ecologically, agreed statements on the

22

Eucharist and even the development of inter-church celebrations may appear trivial and peripheral. The formal *domus Dei* must lift its eyes to the gifts and needs of the whole world about it, the *mundus Dei*, if it would truly worship God. For this God is the God of creation as well as redemption. Church and sacraments, Eucharist supreme among them, must recover their role as *sacramenta mundi*, effective symbols of the divine creative and redemptive activity which cannot be separated into any two-tiered system of sacred and secular. Indeed the fundamental unity of the divine work in creation and redemption is essential to understanding the meaning and centrality of Eucharist for Catholics and all Christians. Only in this setting can the relevance and effectiveness of the Eucharist be maintained and the sacredness, or better, the sacramentality of all creation, cosmic and human, be rediscovered.

WORSHIP AND MORALITY

The unity of creation and redemption applies in a particularly powerful way to the ethical concerns of this chapter.

Worship and morality are intimately linked in the Jewish–Christian tradition. Herein lies the distinctiveness of ethics for Christians that worship and morality constitute two sides of the one human response to Creator/Redeemer and to creation/redeemed. The core of the Catholic tradition of morality in its natural law form depends not primarily on Stoic concepts but on a theology of creation/new creation. The intrinsic and intimate connection between mysticism and morality was finally established in Jesus Christ as 'the way, the truth and the life' (John 14:6).

Word and sacrament, while distinct and yet united in Christ and Church, can be functionally separated in misleading ways. The Reform emphasis on the word has been historically opposed to the Catholic emphasis on sacrament. In the older tradition sacrament could not exist without word and the primary expressions of the word were in Jesus, in the believing community and in the Eucharist. Vatican II and ecumenical dialogue have helped to restore this earlier unity and to renew word for Catholics and sacrament for Reformed ... to a certain extent. A rather different but related opposition has emerged with the development of recent prophetic theologies. Liberation theologies of diverse forms, Latin American, Black and feminist, have seen themselves as primarily theologies of the word. Sacrament fits less easily on to their biblical basis and their political thrust towards radical reform. Indeed actual sacramental practice may be interpreted as endorsing the political status quo and opposed to the liberation and justice sought by the liberationists. In fidelity to their prophetic predecessors in Hebrew tradition and in Jesus, these theologians challenge such sacramental worship as idolatry or magic. The worship of idols, of the false gods of power or money, is the continuing temptation of the powerful and their courtly priests. For the powerless the temptations of magical healing and liberation in place of human analysis and struggle may also co-opt the sacraments to the service of oppression. It is one of the aims of this chapter to expose the prophetic role of the Eucharist and so reinforce the unity in difference of Word and Sacrament.

FRUIT OF THE EARTH

As fruit of the earth, the bread and wine of the Eucharist are rooted in creation, in planet and in cosmos. The cosmic story from the theoretical Big Bang to human consciousness and creativity is traceable in flashback through the elementary and yet highly sophisticated elements of human food and drink employed by Jesus and the Church in the Eucharist. The Creator Spirit drew out of the void and lured into increasingly complex existence the world we acknowledge but have scarcely begun to explore and understand. Despite enormous advances the elusive fundamental particles are more mysterious to contemporary scientists than atoms were to Democritus or protons and electrons to Niels Bohr. And while astronomy and cosmology continue to thrive and to make headlines for lay as well as scientific observers, concepts like 'Big Bang' and 'expanding universe' excite and delight without providing rounded explanation. The list could go on indefinitely. Sciences of matter and mind in their unceasing progress illuminate more and more without necessarily explaining. The growing light they shed emphasizes the larger darkness of origins and purpose, of creativity and freedom, of failure and death. In all this they at once resemble and complement artists, whose insights and creations derive from other angles of vision and other designs of nature. Artistic sense of limit and mystery may resemble that of religion more than that of science. Yet in the religious world of sacrament the discoveries of science and the insights of art can enrich theological attempts to relate sacraments, especially Eucharist, to creation and creativity.

The otherness of creation to Creator, a central mystery for Christians and all believers, is the basis of God's respect for creation. In Genesis terms,

God saw that it was good. God regarded it in its goodness, recognized and respected it as valuable and to be valued. The Creator maintained a communion of respect and care for creation. As God's self-expression made other, creation shares the sacredness of God while being utterly different. Difference in communion characterizes the Creator–creation relationship, although the precise nature of the difference and of the communion will always elude human comprehension.

As creation is respected in its otherness by God; by its very otherness it at once reflects and respects God. By being itself, creation acknowledges its Creator; it implicitly worships God. The developing world of Genesis and of contemporary science, for all their differences, proclaim still more the glory of God. The growing differentiation within the world has over the millennia exposed more deeply its otherness from God and at the same time manifested more fully the inexhaustible riches of God. God's caring regard for this increasing differentiation, leading to life and human life, has received biblical recognition from Genesis to Job to Jesus. 'Behold the lilies of the field . . . ' (Matt 6:28).

Bread and wine as fruit of the earth share in the divine respect for all creation. In the symbolic world of the Eucharist they represent earth and its highly differentiated forms of life and nurture. The divine regard for such life and nurture entered a new phase with Jesus' blessing of the bread and wine, and his giving them to eat and drink as his body and blood. For those who would eat and drink worthily the body and blood of the Lord, the divine regard for earth and its fruits represented by the bread and wine must also receive human expression. Degrading and exploiting the earth with its millions of life forms is to ignore the model of divine respect and to insult the divine gift. Eucharist as recognition and celebration of creation as well as redemption provides the basis and the seal of an ecological ethics. The sacred character of the earth is confirmed in the sacramental elements of the Eucharist. All bread and wine is now seen to be holy and to be respected as such. So is the ground on which we walk. Failure to recognize and live that eucharistic understanding of earth and its gifts is failure to recognize the divine giver also.

WORK OF HUMAN HANDS

All human work presupposes the divine labour of creation. With the emergence of human creativity true collaboration with the creative work of God became possible. Human development of the world of creation becomes co-creation with the Creator God. In that co-operation between divine and human creativity the farming and cooking revolutions led to the development of bread and wine, two of the greatest achievements of divine–human collaboration. The original divine labour of creation and the subsequent divine–human collaboration form essential preparation for the integration of bread and wine, eating and drinking into the great liturgical act of the Eucharist. The divine labour of creation and the human work of co-creation together make up the *praeparatio liturgica* of Christian worship and in particular of the Eucharist. Invitation to the celebration of Eucharist implies invitation to join the *praeparatio*. Inclusion in the Eucharistic celebration should mean inclusion in the work of human hands.

Exclusion from human work is a widespread and depressing feature of our civilization. In Ireland there are 300,000 unemployed, in Britain 3 million, in the European Union 17 to 18 million. Many of these are long-term. Some have never worked at all. Some of the younger will never have a job in their life-time. And this is the more developed and traditionally Christian part of the world. Yet the economic and political system requires the exclusion of so many people from their right to work as recognized in the United Nations Charter, and from exercising their God-given vocation to be co-creators of their world. Can the Eucharist be celebrated in such circumstances without the excluders, the people of economic and political power, eating and drinking judgement on themselves? How can the unemployed be honestly asked to join in celebrating a liturgy from whose preparation in the work of human hands they have been systematically excluded?

SHARING THE MEAL

Divine and human collaboration is always moving beyond the production of food and drink to the creation of a meal, a community event at once celebratory and nourishing. Eucharist is also such an event but in its fuller meaning as eating and drinking bread and wine become body and blood of Christ, it symbolizes the sharing of all humanity in the life-giving gifts of God, including the gift of Godself. Worthy celebration of the Eucharist must again take seriously the full range of its symbolism. The earth and its fruits are for all. The work of human hands and hearts and minds must seek in imitation of the Creator to ensure this. The Eucharist summons Christians to give a lead and play their part in ensuring this, the meal-ministry of Jesus in feeding the hungry and in eating and drinking with sinners and the excluded, provides the background to his farewell meal with his disciples, the origin of our Eucharist. The prophetic questions must once again be voiced. How can we celebrate Eucharist in a world of recurring famine and permanent food mountains and wine lakes? In a world where a billion people live in absolute poverty? In a world where a million children under five die every month in the countries of the South? Given the existing awareness, resources, technology and means of distribution, does the continuing inactivity of the powerful and secure amount to a passive form of genocide? Can we Christians celebrate Eucharist in a genocidal world in which we are at least passive participants?

The prophetic character of the Eucharist inheres in its very sacramentality. The symbolic recognition and celebration include protest and judgement. They summon to resistance and transformation. The range of that summons to judgement and transformation extends as we have seen beyond the *domus Dei* and its individual members or believers to the *mundus Dei*, the natural and human worlds of God. The role of the *domus Dei*, of the Church and of its sacraments is to recognize and promote the transformation of the *mundus Dei* into the *regnum Dei*. From creation to new creation through the coming of the Kingdom is the gift and call of Jesus' redemptive life and death. The Church operates as midwife in this further exercise of divine creativity.

The Church is also under judgement, summoned to transformation itself. In its teaching and living it frequently fails to reflect what it celebrates in Eucharist. Its service to the *regnum Dei*, to the coming of God's Kingdom is thereby diminished. Too often in past and present the Church's explicit or implicit alignment with oppressive powers has contradicted its sacramental enactment of the liberating presence and power of God. Despite all the declarations of fine intentions in papal encyclicals and bishops' pastorals, and the heroic service of so many religious and lay communities and individuals, the Church community constantly stands in need of judgement and conversion. Sometimes the call to judgement may arise outside the Church itself. The *mundus Dei* and its apparent unbelievers may be closer to the *regnum Dei* than the *domus Dei* and its apparent believers. Movement by the Spirit is not limited to the confines of the visible Church. Creation and the larger human community may be at times more effective signs of the coming of the Kingdom. Formal and valid sacraments may be frustrated by ecclesial blindness and weakness.

Oppression of women has for too long been a counter-sign of the coming Kingdom in Church as well as society. Indeed the Church has had to learn from the broader movement towards women's liberation about the extent of that oppression and the need to overcome it. Jesus' exemplary relations with women as recorded in the Gospels seem to have been obscured over the centuries. The eucharistic call for an inclusive society beyond oppressive divisions, including that of male and female (Gal 3:28), is still far from realization. As symbolic meal, underlining the communion aspects of all meals and human gatherings, the Eucharist calls attention to the nurturing and gathering role which women have historically fulfilled. In any future debates about women's role in the celebration of the Eucharist their role at family meals of gathering the family, preparing and serving the food may be ignored only at the expense of the very symbol and sacrament itself.

CELEBRATION AND PROPHECY

The celebratory character of the Eucharist should never be obscured. In the context of creation it echoes God rejoicing in the creation and the creation rejoicing in its God. The 'Mass on the World' vision of Teilhard de Chardin expresses all that magnificently. There remains the judgement and the protest, the 'Mass for hard times' as R. S. Thomas called it. This critical and prophetic vision is finally centred on the Cross. Mass is a sacrifice, Christ's sacrifice re-membered and re-presented. So much of Catholic theology has concentrated on this aspect for so long that the very 'celebration' rang hollow and the social critique was entirely obscured. Yet without the Cross the Mass would not be the Mass. In a world of war and pestilence and starvation, where the slow torture of God and humanity continues as on Calvary, the crucified God is remembered and made present as crucified and identified with all the victims of history. It is also the risen crucified who receives us and whom we receive. Resurrection is cause for celebration but is only available to us as it was to Jesus by taking on the sufferings of the world.

The sign of the Cross can be used to oppress rather than to liberate. Preoccupation with the death on the Cross can become depressing and escapist. Resurrection can be too easily displaced to the end-time. Many Christians, not all women, would welcome more emphasis on birth than on death. New creation is one among many such life-giving images in the New Testament of which 'being born again' is the most obvious. The mystery and the paradox of the life-giving death of Jesus as made present in the Eucharist do not yield to systematic explanation. Eliot's Magi might have had some illuminating comment if they had gone to Calvary rather than to Bethlehem. It may not be impertinent to para- or re-phrase them here.

> Were we led all that way for
> Death or Birth? There was a Death, certainly
> We had evidence and no doubt. I had seen death and birth,
> But had thought they were different . . .

Eucharist is death and birth, fearsome prophecy and joyous celebration.

OTHERNESS IN COMMUNION

The mystery and paradox of the Eucharist inevitably reflect the mystery and paradox of human existence and more broadly still those of the Creator–creation relationship. The otherness characteristic of that relationship, the developing otherness internal to creation itself and the modes of otherness inherent in human relationships transcend our human understanding. In their opacity they signal the fragility of all cosmic and human reality. No thing or person, relationship or community is assured of stability or permanence. The contingency of creaturehood in all its forms and relationships is a matter of everyday experience. Otherness, contingency and their associate, discontinuity, offer a serious challenge to any prospect of community or communion, including eucharistic or Holy Communion.

The assumption of easy communion is deep-rooted in human relationships. Families, neighbourhoods, whole societies and even churches, presume a certain community and solidarity and are often surprised when hostile divisions emerge. That human assumption has its cosmic and even divine analogues. Break-down and division in rock-solid geological formations or the flood of normally trustworthy rivers may suddenly distress human and other inhabitants. The history of God's relationship with humanity is a history of breakdown and distress. God's last hurrah, as it were, in sending God's Son to establish or re-establish community with God's chosen people was apparently no more successful than a long list of previous ones. 'This is the heir . . . let us kill him and the vineyard will be ours' (Mark 12:1ff.). The meal-communities which Jesus established with prostitutes and sinners, tax-collectors and other socially excluded people alienated the religious leaders. His bypassing the Sabbath regulations to heal the sick and feed the hungry offended their sense of the holiness/otherness of God. His claim to overcome the deepest estrangement of all in forgiving sin appeared to them as outright blasphemy. It was an assumption of identity with the divine unnameable holy one, the ultimate other. (In Hebrew 'holy' and 'other' are the same word, as used of Yahweh, the transcendent Other and the Holy One of Israel.)

Jesus' rejection by his people, his betrayal by one of the twelve whom he called personally, his desertion by the others, his condemnation to death by the religious and political authorities and his execution outside the gates of the city as a criminal completed the hostile othering. He was excluded from all community as totally estranged and so dehumanized. The attempts at divine–human communion seem to have finally broken down. Divine and human otherness are no longer open to communion. Discontinuity between God and humanity as between humans themselves prevails. Even the dying Jesus cries out 'My God, my God, why have you forsaken me?' (Matt 27:47).

The estrangement of Jesus, the model of love, in life and death, exposes the range of hostile and destructive division and discontinuity in society and cosmos. Without understanding that, without recognizing our own complicity in it, we cannot hope to go, or better to be taken, beyond it. 'Beyond estrangement' becomes possible for humanity and cosmos in the gracious raising of Jesus from the dead. It becomes accessible in every place and time because on the night before he died:

> As they were eating, Jesus took bread, and blessed, and broke it, and gave it to his disciples and said, 'Take, eat, this is my body'. And he took a cup, and when he had given thanks he gave it to them, saying, 'Drink of it, all of you; for this is my blood of the covenant, which is poured out for many for the forgiveness of sins'. (Matt 26:26–28)

The Holy Communion, which the Eucharist promises and anticipates, involves the disorientation of Calvary. Only those who recognize and take on board the estrangement and discontinuity which Jesus experienced on the Cross can truly enter into new communion with God, neighbour and cosmos. The created otherness and differentiation which in origins and potential reflect the gracious and enriching gifts of the Creator still loom threateningly over our world. The Crucifixion–Resurrection of Jesus exposes both the depth of the threat and the triumph of the gift. A true and holy communion of others in Jesus is what Eucharist symbolizes and realizes. The new creation, however fragile and limited, is emerging in the sharing of bread and wine by his instructions and in his memory. Creator, creation and humanity enjoy new hope of otherness in communion in which differentiation will provide deeper bonds for communication rather than fresh sources of discontinuity and division.

REFERENCES

Tissa Balasuriya, *The Eucharist and Liberation* (Maryknoll, NY: Orbis, 1972).

James B. Dunning, 'Liturgy as prophetic' and Enda McDonagh, 'Liturgy and Christian life' in Peter E. Funk (ed.), *The New Dictionary of Sacramental Worship* (Collegeville, MN/ Dublin: Liturgical Press, 1990).

Elizabeth A. Johnson, *Woman, Earth and Creator Spirit* (Notre Dame, IN: Notre Dame University Press, 1993).

David N. Power, *The Eucharistic Mystery* (Dublin: Gill and Macmillan, 1992).

' . . . and do not hinder them' | 4 |

children, learning and the Eucharist — a perspective from the United Reformed Church

MUCH OF THE WORK of Christiane Brusselmans was committed to enabling children to participate in the Eucharist in a way which is appropriate to their stage of faith development. A similar figure in the URC/Congregational Church was the Rev. H. A. Hamilton. His work followed twenty years of pressure from some parents, church leaders and children for children to be allowed to attend the Eucharist and receive bread and wine. Hamilton was a Congregational minister who, as well as having distinguished ministries in local churches, served for a time as Principal of Westhill College, Birmingham and then as an Assistant General Secretary of the World Council of Churches.

His little book *The Family Church in Principle and Practice*, first published in 1941 with a third edition in 1960, led many in his tradition to re-think the place of children in the church. Family relationships and ways in which children learn in the family circle became the model which the church tried to develop. Hamilton's imagination was provoked by a character in T. S. Eliot's play *The Family Reunion* who says 'I think that the things that are taken for granted at home are more important than all we are taught'. He asked the churches to reflect on what was taken for granted and how their answers to that question related to the gospel. Teaching children was important but the implicit in experience, he argued, was more important, not least because it very often became a part of the subconscious.

By the end of the 1960s there was significant disenchantment with aspects of Hamilton's approach. 'Family' was becoming a much more complex organism. Church people who had not had happy experiences of family life were uneasy about using the family model. Perhaps even more

32

telling was the failure of the model to equip young people to cope with the challenges of life in the world. Many who went away from home and from their home church, to work or to study, found that though they had experienced warmth and loving care, they had not learned a critical approach to faith. They were unable to withstand the cold shafts of questioning, alternative views and cynicism. Nonetheless, Hamilton's work was significant. What was perhaps not recognized in the early period of experimentation was that Hamilton had been profoundly influenced by the Orthodox Church, its liturgy, art and music and by its tradition of administering the Eucharist to newly baptized infants. This bastion of tradition, it might be said, contrasted strongly with the Congregationalism of the day, which was, generally speaking, liberal and eclectic.

THE INFLUENCE OF EDUCATIONAL PSYCHOLOGY

Hamilton's work was part of complementary insights which have been influential in the thinking and practice of the Free Churches[1] in the past 30 years. One source of insight was found in educational psychology. Its high point of influence followed the publication in 1963 of *Readiness for Religion* by Ronald Goldman.[2] This was probably the last serious occasion in which the findings of a research project could be said to apply equally to children in the church and children at school.[3] Schools were soon to be plunged into grappling with the new influx of children representing other world faiths and since the late 1960s teaching in church and religious education in school have very much gone their own ways.[4] More recently, through the work of James Fowler first published in *Stages of Faith: The Psychology of Human Development and the Quest for Meaning*[5] and the more popular and influential *How Faith Grows: Faith Development and Christian Education*,[6] there has been a renewed interest in educational psychology, notably in the stages of faith development.

The other source of insight was broadly based in the sociology of religion and theology and was concerned with the nature of the Church. This was reflected in my own *Learning Community*, published in 1974 and based on the discussion of papers given at a consultation arranged by the World Lutheran Federation and the World Council of Churches. Some of the issues in *Learning Community* and in Hamilton's work were also evident in *The Child in the Church* and *Understanding Christian Nurture*,[7] and were further developed in the Church of England's report *Children in the Way* (1988).

THE PLACE OF CHILDREN

Discussion of the place of children in the Eucharist[8] was on the agendas of some churches in the late 1960s, and during the 1970s numerous local churches, which had the freedom to experiment, were exercising their right. The interest in this subject was probably stirred a little by the use of family as a model of church life, but mainly originated from middle-class parents who were becoming used – not least because of the spread of car ownership – to family activities which included children and parents. By the time of the World Council of Churches' Consultation which led to the publication ... *And Do Not Hinder Them*, there was what might be called a movement in all the mainstream First World Protestant churches for the admission of baptized, but not necessarily confirmed, children to Holy Communion. In most Free Churches children were not admitted to Holy Communion until Confirmation at the age of 12 to 18 years. In ... *And Do Not Hinder Them*, David Holeton[9] shows that there is little that is new in welcoming baptized children to the Eucharist and I was able with ease to obtain pieces written by children in seventeen countries about their experience of doing so. It would be misleading, however, to give the impression that a majority in any denomination had accepted children as full participants at the Holy Table.[10] In the past decade several denominations in Britain have invited their congregations to discuss the matter and some have emphasized the role of parents in helping to decide whether or not their children should receive bread and wine and in answering children's questions. The older Free Church denominations and the Church of Scotland have quietly encouraged their local congregations to have a positive view of the place of children in the Eucharist but none have made the participation of children a policy of their church. Educational material for use in churches has featured the Lord's Supper; among the ecumenical publications the *Partners in Learning* material has been positive in its approach to the participation of children while maintaining a cautious regard for users who hold a different view.[11]

WHAT CHILDREN SAY ABOUT EUCHARIST

Interestingly, perhaps because of an ITV programme on the subject in 1988 more than because of the older publication, I have continued to meet with and to hear from parents who tell me some of the things their children have said about receiving bread and wine. Much of what is reported has a familiar ring about it. Young children still speak about the church's 'sharing service' and about the 'church's party'. Nine- and ten-year-old children speak about being accepted as equals with adults and are moved by the experience of solidarity. Some seemingly perceptive individuals coin intriguing phrases which suggest they have glimpsed an insight which has deep personal meaning, like the nine-year-old Spaniard who wrote about 'going with God to meet him', and the ten-year-old who wrote 'It seems wonderful when a silence falls between everybody in church. The candles spread light so brightly that it almost reminds me of stars on a dark night. When I go up to the altar it gives me a feeling of gladness; something may have come into the world that hasn't been here before.' An eight-year-old Portuguese child wrote of the service as 'a feast of God who is my friend'.

There are still children who feel rejected ('you feel a fool being blessed and just as much a fool staying in your seat') and children who find the language of the liturgy either too difficult or so direct that symbolism and mystery are denied. A three-year-old who heard her minister substitute 'shall live for ever' for the words 'eternal life' buried her face in her mother's lap distraught, saying she did not want to live for ever, no one else did!

In general, it seems that most of what children have to say falls into the categories I used in ... *And Do Not Hinder Them*. Children perceive something of the mystery of the relationship between themselves and God. They believe that receiving bread and wine contributes to their growth in faith; it helps them to think about God and about how they should be expressing their belief. They are moved to look inside themselves, to appreciate their own feelings more and also to look outside themselves and the church. This is expressed in 'Communion is a meal by which God feeds his family. When I go up to the altar I get a very happy feeling in me and it is like being a small child amongst grown-ups having a conversation.' 'When we gave our 1 per cent Appeal so that people in poor countries could grow food I thought that was like sharing communion. When the bread and wine are shared I think of sharing in the world.' This looking out beyond themselves also involves them in thinking about the news, their families and about the story of the church. It seems that the most powerful impact of the service is in giving children a sense of belonging and of the commitment that is associated with belonging. And there are children who perceive that the Eucharist is a very special kind of play.

In summary, the evidence suggests that children between the ages of three and ten years not only have experiences which have meaning and importance for themselves and about which they can write or speak, they can also respond by offering appropriate commitments. By 'appropriate commitments', I mean commitments appropriate to their age and circumstance. We cannot define when commitment begins.

EDUCATION THROUGH THE EUCHARIST

Churches of the Reformation, generally speaking, have been better at cognitive teaching than affective learning. Perhaps in introducing much that they have written with the words 'I feel ... ' children have been reminding us of the importance of the affective dimension of experience. They have known, as John Baillie might have written, with the bottom of their hearts, if not with the top of their minds.[12]

Observation suggests that the order of their experience has been first that through birth and baptism they belong to Christ. Second, they experience that belonging by participating in church life and in the Eucharist with other adults and children. Arising out of this, third, they grow to believe in their belonging; their experience develops from being a subconscious to being a self-conscious activity. Fourth, they acknowledge and profess and reflect upon their understanding of their belonging.

Given this breadth of background and of apparent interest, it is a matter of concern that the churches have used children's experience so little and made so limited a use of the Eucharist as part of an educational process. For instance, the celebration is essentially a community or corporate activity. The proper location of the sharing, taking the upper room as a model, is among a group of people who have learned to be humble, to forgive and love, care for and respect each other and who also have a common purpose, however ill defined that might be. That is, the occasion of the celebration affords the church an opportunity to pause and to explore the meaning of Christian community, the values of the community and the purpose or aims of the community.

Much has been written, for instance in *The Child in the Church*, about the 'place' of children in the church. They have a place by virtue of their baptism. Those who have not been baptized have a place by right of creation and redemption. The pastoral and social consequences of this have greatly exercised church people, as may be seen in several of the publications mentioned above. Attention should now turn away from a discussion of 'place' and be given to the 'role' of children – and people of any age – in the Christian community. In a co-operative and participative style of church life their role would be that of being active in co-operation, as resource people, friends, supporters, questioners, as witnesses and the witnessed to, instigators of celebration and part of the celebration. Even to compile so partial a list is to raise questions about the capacity of congregations to take seriously the nature of their being together around the Holy Table.

In many Third World contexts, where the participation of the children in the Eucharist is not an issue, the children of the church sometimes have a richer experience of community than do children in the West who share in the central communal act. In the struggle to survive, children know they not only have a place, they know they have a role and unless they fulfil their role their family or village or wider community will be impoverished. In the Western church there is also impoverishment when children do not fulfil their role. But because churches have never learned to live with the riches that are theirs, they do not notice their impoverishment. It is the person coming in from outside to whom the charade of community is most clearly evident. The churches speak of the Kingdom, they claim to witness to the values of the Kingdom, they celebrate the gift of the Kingdom, they demonstrate the birth and nature of the Kingdom around a Holy Table, but the community life of the church falls short of being a foretaste of what is both a gift to the church and part of its creative task. The community of the church should offer children an experience which convinces them that it is a sign of the Kingdom in the process of liberation.

THE EUCHARIST AS ACTION

The Eucharist is also essentially an action: there has to be taking and breaking, pouring and sharing, and receiving. Every participant can see that action is a part of the celebration. Experience of activity-based learning in lower schools or of action-based research in higher education suggests that the action of the Lord's Supper affords the church a vast learning opportunity. The actions of the Lord's Supper are both liturgical and symbolic of the actions of daily life; they are both personal and political. So it is appropriate to explore what they mean for daily life. How is it that breaking is creative? What does sharing mean when the poor pray, give us this day our daily bread? What does it mean to receive? How is the local church community involved in the political acts of breaking and sharing, giving and receiving? Perhaps the church, with children as a part of it, would be a more significant Christian community if it were involved more in 'secular' eucharistic action. Anyone who visited Nicaragua in the years following the revolution can hardly fail to have been impressed by the social engagement of the children. This was especially true of those who, perhaps aged only six or seven years, had mothers and fathers who were involved in the overthrow of the dictator and of those who had done their bit as messengers and carriers of food. To hear some of these children speaking about the future of their country and how they hoped to contribute to it was to encounter a depth of theological discussion and of Christian social vision not commonly experienced in Britain. Participation in the action and reflection on the action had been their decisive mentor.

Action takes place in a context: part of the learning process for children is that of making sense of their context, discovering how to handle some of the issues it raises and seeing some relationships and wider implications. For the church the immediate context is the local issues and ways in which national and international policies impact on them. The 1986 Vatican Instruction on *Christian Freedom and Liberation*[13] outlined the wider context of the churches' thinking and action: the ecological crisis, individualist ideology, relations between rich and poor countries, international finance, benefits accruing from sciences, mastery over nature by means of science and technology, wars and the threat of wars. Children who watch television news inhabit this world of global issues and from a young age have views about it and about the ways in which adults behave. They also inhabit a more immediate world of family and home, school and playground, where love and jealousy, birth and death, poverty and plenty, acceptance and rejection have to be handled. The experience of children is a well from which children, as well as adults, must draw in the course of the spiritual life.[14] The context of the church and the child is where the values of the Eucharist find meaning and the way of the Cross becomes a reality.

AUTHENTIC VALUES

The relation of the values demonstrated and implicit in the Eucharist – giving, breaking, receiving, sharing, participating, equality – to society at large raises vast questions. Does the church celebrate and hold its values as a ghetto in a plural society? Does the church speak only to individuals, and not to society as a whole? What is the relation between public worship and public life? How do these values relate to institutional life, for instance, the life of the church or the school or to places of work or to financial policies? It is because of an absence of any positive answer to such questions as these that many children and young people are frustrated by the church. The disparity between public utterance and public life, between piety and politics, leaves them feeling that the church is serious only about maintaining a ritual. Such issues can be explored only through thoughtful and informed conversation, dialogue between people who may hold different views, openness to one's neighbour and an attitude of inclusiveness rather than of exclusiveness. The Upper Room was a place of conversation and argument: that is what its remembrance offers as a third learning opportunity to children in the church. The church's offer of redemption and the world's struggle for self-emancipation must be brought together.

The argument is in danger of becoming circular: if there is no developing experience of community, there is unlikely to be any significant conversation. If there is no opportunity for taking action together, conversation is likely to be forced. If there is no conversation, no plans for actions and meaningful community can exist. These three learning opportunities which, I suggest, grow out of Holy Communion belong together. They are all aspects of the one celebration and the one task. They facilitate that central task of Christian education, doing and living theology.

CHILDREN CHALLENGE US

Thus the participation of children in the Eucharist is a challenge to the church to be and to become. The readiness with which children express their views about their experience suggests that they are ready for the celebration to be the starting point of something new. There has to be dialogue – taking and giving, pouring out and receiving – for teaching to be within the intellectual range of children and within their context. Nor is there anything in adult education to suggest that adults have different needs in this regard. Perhaps above all what is at issue is the integrity of the church – community, action, and conversation are integral to the nature of the celebration – and integrity in the use of Scripture. Readings from the Bible are often concluded with a phrase such as 'this is the word of the Lord'. Many children and adults have learned enough to know that the phrase at least begs questions. It would be more true to say: this is the word of editors, or of an early church, or of a faithful and pious Jew. Yet many people have found that parts of the Bible become the word of the Lord as they have wrestled honestly and openly with an aspect of their experience and brought the Bible, with relevant modern scholarship, to bear as a resource. This dialogue between the word and experience which had led to the finding of the Word has been well rehearsed.[15] It is my contention that the same dialogue is necessary for children truly to discover with continuing integrity that the Altar, the Holy Table, the Communion Table, is the table of the Lord. And there we may be privileged to experience a radical revolutionary firing of the churches which the world and the churches so desperately need.

NOTES

1. Hamilton's influence was mainly in the Congregational and Presbyterian Churches which later became the United Reformed Church, and the Baptist and Methodist Churches.
2. Ronald Goldman, *Readiness for Religion* (London: Routledge and Kegan Paul, 1963). Goldman was also a Congregational minister and had been a member of Hamilton's staff at Westhill.
3. When during the 1970s and 1980s churches began to develop 'all-age' learning, it was quickly seen that some of Goldman's findings did not apply to children who were learning as equals with adults. In mixed-age groups some of the limitations of perception associated with peer group learning were not so rigid.
4. Between Goldman and the development of the teaching of world faiths, there was a brief period of influence for Harold Loukes, *Teenage Religion* (London: SCM Press, 1961), the product of another research project which emphasized the importance of teaching based in life experience.
5. James Fowler, *Stages of Faith: The Psychology of Human Development and the Quest for Meaning* (New York: HarperCollins, 1976).

6. *How Faith Grows: Faith Development and Christian Education* (London: National Society/Church House Publishing, 1991).

7. *The Child in the Church* (London: British Council of Churches, 1976); *Understanding Christian Nurture* (London: British Council of Churches, 1981).

8. I have used Eucharist, Holy Communion and Lord's Supper interchangeably as synonyms reflecting the practices of the Roman Catholic and mainstream Protestant Churches. The issue of children attending the Eucharist was not so urgent in the Catholic Church since children tended to be confirmed at the beginning of their junior school years, though what the service meant to them was an issue, at least for some. The Anglican Church tended to confirm in the early teens and the Free Churches in the middle or later teens. The issue for the churches in the Anglican, Methodist and Reformed communions was whether children who had been baptized but not confirmed could receive bread and wine. A new emphasis was placed on baptism being the normal mode of entry into the church, on the Lord's Supper as being part of the nurturing of Christian discipleship and on confirmation as being an appropriate marking of adult commitment.

9. Now Professor Holeton. See his paper, 'The Communion of infants and young people', p. 59, and my paper, 'Children and Holy Communion', p. 24, in Geiko Müller-Fahrenholz (ed.), *. . . And Do Not Hinder Them: An Ecumenical Plea for the Admission of Children to the Eucharist* (Geneva: World Council of Churches, 1982).

10. Again, as with Eucharist, Holy Communion and Lord's Supper, though the theology behind the terms differs, I use Holy Table and Altar interchangeably.

11. *Partners in Learning* provides material for use week by week as a basic church education programme with children and adults. It is published by a Protestant ecumenical consortium and is used mainly in Methodist, Reformed, Baptist and Anglican churches.

12. John Baillie, *Our Knowledge of God* (London: Oxford University Press, 1952).

13. 22 March 1986: English text published by the Catholic Truth Society (London, 1986).

14. This is a phrase of Bernard of Clairvaux.

15. For instance in H. Cunliffe Jones, *The Authority of the Biblical Revelation* (London: James Clarke, 1945).

A vision for catechesis in the 1990s

5

DAMIAN LUNDY FSC

ONE OF THE OUTSTANDING CONTRIBUTIONS of catechetical pioneers like Christiane Brusselmans was to inspire fellow practitioners with a transforming vision of the potential of catechesis to change the Church and the world. 'Catechesis', she wrote in 1977, 'is not only transmitting religious knowledge to students during a religion class. It involves the master who addresses disciples so that by, through and beyond Christian instruction the master transmits a way of life, a vision that is the life of faith.'[1] After a brief examination of what catechesis is and why it is important, this essay will offer an outline of some important twentieth-century developments in catechetics. Finally, after some observations about the contemporary social context of catechesis, I shall conclude by offering a few suggestions about contemporary catechetical needs.

1. Catechesis is the process by which Christian faith is nurtured and educated. It is, and always has been, a key mission and ministry in the Church, because, in the words of Jacques Audinet, catechesis is 'the church building the church in a given culture'.[2] The reason why there cannot be any one approach to catechesis, fixed for all time, is because 'to live is to change': societies develop, cultures change, new needs become apparent, and the Church has to respond to new challenges. The alternative is to become a museum, to get stranded in the past, to become fossilized.

Only a very simplistic view of catechesis will see it as the straightforward, unchanging proclamation of a message fixed for all time. The most significant twentieth-century catechetical thinkers have emphasized the double fidelity that catechesis involves: fidelity to the God whose word Christians are called to announce, and fidelity to the needs of those with whom catechists and teachers share the Christian message. This concept of a 'double fidelity' was especially emphasized by French catechetical pioneers earlier in this century, notably by Fr Joseph Colomb (1902–79), who did so much to encourage the professional formation of catechists and, in his later years, to develop approaches to adult catechesis. But it is part of the British Catholic catechetical tradition too, as is evident from F. H. Drinkwater's very first editorial in *The Sower* (June 1919):

> We have started this paper not only because we believe that there is a real call amongst Catholic teachers for something of the kind, but also because we believe that education is the point on which all earnest Catholics ought to concentrate their attention at present. Of the many points of contact between the Church and the modern world, education is the point where Catholicism has most to gain by energetic thought and action, and most to lose by an atmosphere of indifference and we wish to persuade all our fellow Catholics of this ... Another thing: this paper has no official character whatever. It makes no claim to speak for any Catholic authorities, nor for the Catholic body in general. We regard ourselves perhaps as a kind of forward patrol exploring what is largely new ground and sending back reports and suggestions to the main body ...[3]

This twentieth-century view of the catechist's prophetic mission is rather startling: the reference to 'new ground' suggests likely difficulties, misunderstandings and dangers. A glance at the history of catechetics shows that there has been no shortage of these.

It was Tertullian (*c.* 200) who, arguing against infant baptism, wrote 'Christians are *made*, not born'. And this is surely true. Even if a baby is baptized into the Christian community, she or he will not automatically grow into an adult Christian, without being nurtured and educated in the beliefs and values of the Christian community. No one was more convinced of this than Christiane Brusselmans. An essential aspect of this personal formation in faith, hope and love will be to help individuals and communities see the relevance of faith to life. The important and well-prepared 1977 Synod on Catechesis stated: 'It is not possible today to conceive or develop catechetical programmes in a way which is only a deepening of abstract truths formulated in a fixed, once-for-all manner ...

through catechesis, the Christian faith must become incarnate in all cultures.'[4]

From this perspective, to start any new catechetical initiative is to undertake a new adventure. It is bound to involve (in Drinkwater's words) 'exploring what is largely new ground', what the 1968 international catechetical conference at Medellín called 'taking on the function of laboratories and testing-grounds for investigation'.[5] Those entrusted with initiatives like the establishment of new catechetical projects need the support and trust of the leaders of the local church, since they play a key role in influencing its future, and, hopefully, their mission will also affect the future of the wider local community. Unfortunately, experience shows that such trust has often been lacking.

It is beyond the scope of the present article to offer even a rudimentary historical sketch of the tumultuous developments which have marked the history of the catechetical movement in the universal and local church during the twentieth century. What I can do is to present five important developments which affect the nature of the task which faces those responsible for catechesis in the local church today.

2.1 The twentieth century has seen a major shift in emphasis from a preoccupation with the religious instruction of children in classrooms, by teachers using catechisms, to a broader understanding of catechesis as *a life-long process of growth in personal faith*, in which communities are challenged to accept responsibility for the education of all their members, young and old. The movement is a parallel development to changes in secular education in our society, which now extends for many people beyond the age of five to 16. It makes great demands on the local church's resources, in terms of personnel and finance, because it means that, while children are not to be neglected, a diocese cannot put all its eggs into one basket. This was accepted by the Bishops' Conference of England and Wales at the National Pastoral Congress in 1980 and by the subsequent adoption of the ever-expanding National Project of Catechesis and Religious Education, on which it was my privilege to work as a co-ordinator for several years.[6] The underlying vision of the Project is of a cradle-to-grave ministry in a variety of contexts and settings.

2.2 The General Catechetical Directory of 1971 accepted that '*adult catechesis*, since it deals with persons who are capable of an adherence that is fully responsible, must be considered the chief form of catechesis' (GCD

20). This conclusion was not quite as revolutionary as it has sometimes been presented. St Pius X, Pope from 1903 to 1914, and very committed to catechesis, stressed in his encyclical *Acerbo Nimis* (April 1905) the universal importance of the ministry of catechesis for the Church of his day: Pius was concerned about 'the vast numbers, and they are constantly increasing, who are utterly ignorant of the truths of religion, among all ages and classes of people'. His proposed solution was regular and systematic teaching of the Catechism. The encyclical set out plainly six precepts to introduce uniformity of practice throughout the universal Church. Five were directed towards the instruction of children and young people; the sixth referred to the 'regular instruction of adults on days of obligation in easy style, suited to the intelligence of their hearers, at such time of the day ... most convenient for the people, but not during the hour in which the children are taught'. The textbook for these classes, divided systematically over a four- or five-year period, was the Catechism of the Council of Trent.[7]

This is exactly what one might have expected of the apostolically-minded Pius X, even from the well-known motto which described the aims of his pontificate: 'to restore all things in Christ'. But the Pope's model of education was unmistakably a transmission model, and his understanding carried no awareness of the limitations of the Tridentine (or Roman) Catechism. In 1956, Drinkwater, a great admirer of Pius X's zeal but a critic of his intransigent attitude towards adult questioning (as expressed most forcefully in the condemnation of 'modernism', a term perhaps coined by the Pope himself), wrote an article 'On the making of catechisms'. In this he noted that the Roman Catechism had never really fulfilled the hope of its originators by reaching adult Catholics every Sunday. 'The theology was spread too thick, the book was too unwieldy, the sentences too lengthy, the whole effort of adaptation too much for the ordinary priest.'[8] Those who place too much hope in too simplistic a use of the English (1994) text of the *Catechism of the Catholic Church* might take note of this warning.[9]

Adult catechesis, in common with all forms of adult education, has to take very seriously the *experience and questions* of those to whom it is offered, if it is to be in any way effective. Here is an obvious application of the 'double fidelity' principle described earlier. Simple transmission methods – what Brian Wicker called 'the theology of the gramophone'[10] – will always be inadequate. If these methods failed in 1905, they will most certainly fail in 1995, not only because the technology of the gramophone has given way to that of the more sophisticated compact disc player, but because modern hearers of the word are even less likely to accept what is fed to them without questioning it in the light of their experience. Some talk about the need for the experience of authority to give way to the primary authority of personal experience. To many Catholics, this may sound very Protestant.

In 1965, Alphonso Nebreda published a book called *Kerygma in Crisis?* in which he called for a radical reappraisal of the Church's entire pastoral approach – a move from a view of Church in which the majority of Catholics were those baptized in infancy to one centred on adults who knowingly and willingly present themselves to the Church and ask for baptism. The change implied 'an honest scrutiny of our adult Catholics', declared Nebreda: 'How many of our baptized people have been evangelized? How many have ratified the commitment to Christ which others made in their name at baptism? . . . Far from dispensing us from further work, baptism demands that we help our children toward an ever more personal and mature act of faith.'[11] This was a prophetic call during the era of Vatican II for adult catechesis to become not some kind of optional luxury but a necessity in the Church. The council itself, discussing the responsibility of bishops for catechesis in their dioceses, had asked that instruction in faith be given to 'children, adolescents, young people and *even* adults' (*Christus Dominus* 14). Not perhaps a very convincing explicit call, though the implicit call for an educated adult church is to be found scattered throughout all the important documents of Vatican II.[12] It became more explicit in many post-conciliar documents like those deriving from synods of the Latin American church, and, closer to home, in the report of the 1980 National Pastoral Congress in Liverpool.

2.3 Catechesis is concerned with the nurture and education of *faith*. In the words of Berard Marthaler, 'Catechesis speaks not merely to the mind but to the whole person. Catechesis is education *in* the faith, not merely instruction *about* the faith.'[13] An important development, which catechists now take for granted, has been a gradual move from much emphasis on the intellectual understanding of faith (what one might call 'head faith') to a broader appreciation of the experiential dimensions of 'heart faith' (the effect faith has on our relationship with God and with our fellow human beings) and 'hands faith' (the effects of our beliefs on our actions and behaviour). Religious education in secondary schools is sometimes criticized today for placing too much emphasis on the experiential dimension to the neglect of the intellectual. Edward Schillebeeckx begins one of his books by writing 'Believers are persons who think and who are in history. Their faith causes them to think.'[14] Surely the important thing here must be to balance the three dimensions and, in our enthusiasm for, say, appropriate behaviour or attitudes, not to neglect the intellectual side.

During the twentieth century, the gradual shift from the use of the word 'catechism' to describe the task of religious education to the more common use of the older term 'catechesis' is relevant and important. To be fully alive, Christians need maturity of personal faith, which will follow partly from education as 'meaningful learning' rather than as 'cognitive teaching' of abstract doctrine, and partly from the inspiration of the Holy Spirit, to which education seeks to open those to whom it is offered. Drinkwater, consistently critical of the 'penny catechism', had a witty way of referring to the excesses he fought against when he described a prescription of unadulterated Denzinger as a stiff whisky and soda without very much soda. It is good to remember that Canon Drinkwater's considerable catechetical accomplishments were sparked off by his experience as a young chaplain of ministering to young soldiers in the First World War. Here he encountered the phenomenon of what he called the 'leakage', the abandonment of religious practice by these young people: 'It was clear that their religion had never really got into their mind, and not much into their heart', he wrote. 'The catechism, learned as they had learned it, had never come to mean anything to them. The only part of their instruction which had lasted was the practical part, and even of that the effects were sometimes spoilt by unfortunate mental associations ("Had enough of that when I was at school, Father!").'[15]

2.4 It is hardly necessary to draw attention to a wonderful development in the Church since Vatican II, and truly a fruit of that council's renewal: I mean the expansion of *ministries* in the Church, and the significant move from a view of ministry as restricted to clergy and religious to a growing conviction that all Christians are called to collaborative ministries of various types, since the entire Church is entrusted with the task of mission and evangelization. In the words of St John Baptist de La Salle (1651–1719) – who provides a memorably inspiring description of that churchy word 'evangelization' – 'God has chosen you to make him known to others'.[16] De La Salle's 'you' was originally addressed to his 'brothers', but these days we have, by the grace of the Holy Spirit, developed a richer, more inclusive understanding of ministry which embraces all the people of God. In the words of Pope Paul VI:

> It is with the greatest of joy that we see a multitude of pastors, religious and lay people who, in their zeal for the task of preaching Christ, are seeking constantly to improve the proclamation of the gospel. We fully approve the open approach which the Church of our time has adopted in pursuance of this objective. There is an openness to reflection, first of all, and then an openness to ecclesial ministries capable of renewing and strengthening the vigour of our evangelization.[17]

To this one might add the visionary words of Pope John Paul II:

> The eyes of faith behold a wonderful scene: that of a countless number of lay people, both men and women, busy at work in their daily life and activity, often far from view and quite unacclaimed by the world, unknown to the world's great personages but nonetheless looked upon in love by the Father, untiring labourers who work in the Lord's vineyard. Confident and steadfast through the power of God's grace, these are the humble yet great builders of the Kingdom of God in history.[18]

2.5 Any consideration of the twentieth-century scene in catechesis must be struck by one obvious characteristic: the fact that the involvement of leading pioneering figures has been distressingly marked by *misunderstanding*, suffering and suspicion – from within as well as from outside the established Church. Drinkwater himself, always outspoken about the inadequacies of the catechism, remained until his death a controversial figure in the eyes of many church leaders, as did many theologians and biblical scholars in the first decade of the century, who sought to relate religious belief and practice to life in modern society. So did Jungmann and his contemporaries who pioneered the kerygmatic movement in the Church of the 1930s in Germany: advocating a rediscovery of the origins and sources of Christianity, they argued (in Marthaler's words) that 'more is required of Christian education than the handing on of shop-worn formulas, tired customs, and trite devotions'.[19] An English translation of Jungmann's 1936 book *The Good News and Our Proclamation of Faith* was not permitted until 1962. In the French Church of the 1940s and 1950s,

Colomb, Coudreau and their contemporaries suffered misunderstanding and even persecution from the official Church when they emphasized the need to respect the psychological stages of child development, and sought to reintroduce into modern, secularized, Western society the adult cate-chumenate.[20] H. J. Richards and his Corpus Christi collaborators in England in the 1970s were enthusiastic about the new freedoms and opportunities introduced by Vatican II, though this enthusiasm ensured many clashes with Church authorities. Many of the figures I have mentioned were blacklisted by the Vatican. And my account would not be complete without a mention of the architects of the National Project of Catechesis in England and Wales in the 1990s, who are keen to provide children and adolescents with a religious education relevant in a sec-ularized and multi-faith society, though their aims are often misunderstood and their motives are frequently questioned.

It is also especially important to note the distinctive contributions of several *women* catechetical pioneers in this century, whose place in the modern history of catechetics has not been sufficiently recognized. I have in mind French practitioners like Marie Fargues, Françoise Derkenne and others; in England early supporters of Drinkwater's *Sower* initiatives like A. M. Scarre and V. C. Barclay, and women associated with Corpus Christi College like Sisters Rena, Romain and Margaret of Jesus (Ruth Duck-worth). One of the most influential of all was Christiane Brusselmans. In his tribute to her, James Parker (who worked with her at Leuven as well as in the USA) emphasized what her many admirers and imitators appre-ciated: words used in the RCIA text like conversion, catechesis, church, liturgy and sacrament were 'revolutionary notions' challenging Christians to translate their implications into formative experiences which 'renew the church from the ground up'.[21] 'What I wish would emerge' from the 1977 Synod on Catechesis, she wrote, 'is the importance of the child's faith communities.' That would involve a journey from religious instruction to Christian initiation, from intellectual knowledge to 'a way of life, a vision that is the life of faith'. As a highly effective international communicator and influential pastoral theologian, Christiane knew (and only her closest friends appreciated this) that the cost of her visionary sensitivity and giftedness lay in the unbelievably dark and agonizing depressions which affected her throughout her life (as they had affected previous generations of her family) and eventually cost Christiane her life.

There is no scope here to examine the rights and wrongs of individual controversies, but it is surely worth noting the important contribution made by pioneers of the catechetical movement to the reform and renewal of the Church's life and mission whose visionary work bore fruit during the Second Vatican Council. The fruit grew among thorns. I was struck by the fateful remark included in the introduction written by H. J. Richards and Peter de Rosa to the 1967 English edition of Gabriel Moran's *God Still Speaks*. 'Moran', they wrote, 'shows that there is no such thing as catechetics without tears, that it is even more difficult to be a Christian teacher than it is to be a Christian.'[22]

3. Reference to the often pain-filled task of building the Kingdom of God in 'history' provides a way into another point in this sketchy account of the renewal of catechesis in our century: the greater importance now attached to the *social context* of catechesis and evangelization – that 'given culture' to which I have referred, which is where evangelization and catechesis take place and which necessarily has an important influence on both the content of the message and the approach of the messengers.

Paragraph 7 of the 1988 Roman document on the *Religious Dimension of Education in a Catholic School* notes: 'The Council provided a realistic analysis of the religious condition of the world today, and paid explicit attention to the special situation of young people; educators must do the same.'[23] The reference here is to sections 4–10 of the Pastoral Constitution on the Church in the Modern World, a reminder of how *Gaudium et Spes* describes the signs of the times – in other words, of how it analyses modern society. In speaking of the fundamental and rapid changes which affect our way of thinking and acting, the council talks about a 'social and cultural transformation'. This, we are told, is accompanied by an increase in uncertainty and anxiety, and by a growing awareness of needs and divisions in society. There is a concern to improve the temporal order without comparable spiritual progress. The social changes evident in the 1960s included notable technological changes (symbolized by space research, as well as by advances in biological, physiological and social sciences). These changes were matched by changes in the social order, such as the extensive spread of urban industrial society, and advances in social communication, with a resulting growth in forms of freedom of expression. We are moreover told that the condition of the modern world poses a challenge to inherited institutions and ways of thinking, with a consequent growth in unbelief and religious indifference. As well as noting the growing sense of *global* identity, the Constitution referred to an increasing awareness of imbalances and conflicts, especially in regard to social justice issues (e.g., the contrast between rich and poor in world society, inequalities between men and women, and in the sphere of education). Yet, given the impact of secularism on our world, for people faced with the evolution of modern society the basic urgent questions still arise: 'What is man and woman? What is the meaning of suffering, evil and death which persist even in the midst of such progress? ... What can people contribute to society or expect from society? What comes after this earthly existence?'[24]

In response to this situation, the Church 'believes that the key and focus and culmination of all human history are to be found in its Lord and Master', the Risen Christ, who is the same yesterday, today and tomorrow, and in whose light the mystery of humankind may be elucidated. We are also assured, in a memorable phrase which all catechists should recognize, that 'the future of humanity lies in the hands of those who are strong enough to provide coming generations with reasons for living and hoping' (GS 34).

Thirty years after Vatican II, the social context in which we catechists work has become even more complex. In an attempt to offer a broad perspective of the 1990s I point to seven characteristics: (1) socio-political changes which have changed our world order (e.g., the collapse of communism and the growth of the European Community); (2) the extensive new ecological awareness which affects the way most people, not only Christians, view the world and its resources; (3) the growth of social conservatism in many parts of the world, and (4) the new fundamentalism, as reflected in the ever-growing new religious movements; (5) the experience for us all of life in a multi-cultural and multi-faith society, brought into our living-rooms through the ever more influential forces of modern technology; (6) the impact of various liberation movements on social traditions and personal values; (7) renewed emphasis on the importance of the experiential in human life. Christians may not approve of all these influences, but they pose a major challenge to catechesis and evangelization in our world, since they profoundly affect the people who live in it. We ignore any of them at our peril.

A concluding part of this essay will raise questions about contemporary catechetical needs. It will mention seven points, without commenting on any of them in detail. (Readers may be reminded of the long-winded preacher who brought relief to his congregation after 25 minutes of rather heavy theology by saying 'And so, brethren, I come to my final point: the fruits of the redemption' – only to dash their hopes when he added 'These are elevenfold!').

4.1 Any tribute to Christiane Brusselmans must begin by noting that a priority for any diocese which takes the Decade of Evangelization seriously must be to develop the *Rite of Christian Initiation of Adults* in its parishes. The exciting opportunities which helped to transform catechesis and ministry in many dioceses in the 1980s, especially following the symposium organized by Christiane at Senanque in June 1978, may now be less new, but they ought not to be less innovative or less available. Certain pastoral problems which affect some inquirers (notably difficult marriage situations) mean that the catechumenate needs continuing research. And experience of successful RCIA initiatives always whets the appetite of other members of the community, enticing them to play an active part in the practice of various ministries in their community.

4.2 This may sound like a cliché but surely a key priority for any diocese must be to look to the needs of *adolescents and young adults*, so many of whom become disillusioned with the Church which seems to have little to offer them, and which may even appear to them to have no need of them. There is a tendency to leave this problem to our secondary schools, but, as Christiane constantly maintained, it continues to be a major unresolved problem for the entire Catholic community. It calls for the attention of concerned apostles in homes, parishes, schools and other groupings.

No fewer than four Vatican departments co-operated some years ago to produce a report, *New Religious Movements: A Challenge to the Church*. The welcome and original feature of this report was its willingness to look critically at the Catholic Church, which many young people reject in favour of new religious or pseudo-religious movements. The report, published in an abbreviated version by the CTS,[25] sees these movements not so much as a *threat* to the Church but as a *challenge*. It asks why young people join new religious movements and answers the question with reference to nine factors: the need to belong; the search for answers; the search for wholeness; the search for cultural identity; the need to feel special; the search for transcendence; the need for spiritual guidance; the need for vision; the need to be involved. These are the very areas to which youth retreat centres seek to give attention. So must every diocese. Now is it entirely unreasonable to suggest that our Church, if truly a community of the disciples of the Christ who came that we may have life and have it to the full, ought to be able to satisfy for its young people at least some of their deeper desires? Contemplating young people, the report says 'There is a vacuum crying out to be filled. One reason for the success of the new movements has been the failure of the Church to respond adequately to new needs and aspirations; if the Church does now take up the challenge posed by the emergence of these movements they may yet prove to have been the stimulus to spiritual renewal and a revitalization of its pastoral practice.'[26]

4.3 Another group which demands urgent pastoral attention in Britain today is the increasing number of people in our society who are *elderly*. Their spiritual and material needs are evident. If 'to live is to change', there are many who do so with great difficulty, many who feel lonely, many who need pastoral care to cope with the challenges of this final stage of their pilgrimage. Life for many (and among the many I include several elderly priests and religious) can be a crisis of faith, hope and love. Perhaps our religious communities could use their enormous resources of elderly sisters and brothers to share with their contemporaries 'reasons for living and hoping'. Could the various diocesan pastoral centres develop a new apostolate by encouraging our parishes to respond generously to the needs and aspirations of the elderly?

4.4 The 'vacuum crying out to be filled' for the young, and that phrase from Vatican II, 'reasons for living and hoping', point, I suggest, to needs and desires which are real for people in every part of our society, whether they are old or young. In several ways, the phrase provides a good definition of *spirituality*, the relevance of faith to life. There is a memorable phrase of Nietzsche, quoted by Victor Frankl in his vivid 1946 reflection on his observations and experiences in Auschwitz: 'The person who has a *why* to live for can bear with almost any *how*.' As Frankl wrote, 'Woe to him who saw no more sense in his life, no aim, no purpose, and therefore no point in carrying on. He was soon lost.' A loss of faith in the future is a loss of spiritual hold, and it can affect people of any age, especially those who have been hit by failure or disillusionment. There is no shortage of either in our society. Surely our specialist catechetical centres are called to be a catalyst for the network of parishes and other groups which make up the local church and which are called to evangelize society today.

4.5 Development of a deeper spirituality will also lead to a renewed appreciation of the variety of *vocations* which make up the Christian life.

The existence of diverse ministries points to many different vocations, which exist not in competition but so as to function collaboratively in the Church.

4.6 A final word about *conflict*, which, as I showed earlier, has been an unfortunate aspect of the catechetical movement. Earlier in the century, Baron von Hügel analysed the role played in religion by three elements which often cause tension, since, although all three are necessary in any Christian community, they tend almost necessarily to conflict. These are the *institutional*, the *critical* and the *mystical* elements.[27] In a recent book on the difficulties which challenge religious life today, Sister Evelyn Woodward shows how the roles of poet, prophet and pragmatist tend to conflict in religious communities or provinces. The religious who embody these gifts embody contrasting values, all of which are necessary for a truly holistic understanding of religious life; since 'pragmatists who are seized by the vision of the poets and impelled by the energy of the prophets are men and women who can see patterns and produce programs not in a merely businesslike way ... but in a manner that is deeply respectful, careful and creatively in touch with the insights of their companion leaders'.[28] The solution to the tensions which result would appear to lie in balanced communities, where potentially conflicting interests are respected, and where 'the combined personal and communal gifts of poetry, prophecy and pragmatism are called for' and appreciated. But I suggest that our pastoral centres ought above all to promote the gifts of poetry and prophecy, and that their particular contribution to a diocese will be to provide vision and inspiration.

4.7 If the dominant model of the Church today is to be that of a community of disciples and apostles of Jesus Christ, moved by his Spirit, it will value diversity and encourage creativity, since both will favour and energize *mission*.

5. It seems appropriate to conclude this essay with a quotation from Canon Drinkwater (1886–1982). In 1965, reflecting on the as yet unpublished Pastoral Constitution on the Church in the Modern World, this great English pioneer (then aged 79) showed the breadth of his vision:

> If Schema 13 gets through the Council with a large majority ... it
> will evidently only be achieved through pasting paper over a lot of

big cracks, and the paper will not last long. Does it seem too unrealistic then to suppose that the faithful of the future will be expected to use their own moral judgement much more than in the past? And that all our schools above primary level will have to undertake serious training in Christian freedom and the meaning and education of the personal conscience? Our bishops and clergy, instead of laying down the law in every circumstance of life, will often say something like: 'On this matter there is no agreement yet in the Church; the best book giving both sides of the question is so and so, you can read both sides, or if you don't read you can ask the advice of somebody whose judgment you respect: and then make up your own mind in the sight of God.' To the more authoritarian type of cleric this may seem at first like the end of the world. But to the eye of humble faith it may look like what Pope John and Pope Paul have predicted for the Church: a second Pentecost, heralding a fresh renewal of the face of the earth.[29]

Arising from this essay are three questions:

(1) Given the agreement about the necessity and obvious importance of catechesis, must it continue to arouse so much *controversy*?
(2) Why is catechesis a ministry for the *whole community*, which can never simply be taken over by any one group (e.g. theologians, clergy, 'experts')?
(3) As we approach the millennium, what can *we* learn from the rather complicated history of the catechetical movement in the twentieth century?

There are, of course, many other questions, but the main purpose of this essay has been to remind readers that, in the words of Christiane Brusselmans, 'the purpose of catechesis is to initiate people into the living faith of the Church. It is a question of a faith of conversion, of interiority, of communion and of search for meaning. It is a question of leading them beyond the visible, audible and conceptual signs to the threshold of the mystery of God.'[30]

NOTES

This essay is an expanded version of the Thévenet lecture delivered to a gathering at the RE Centre of the diocese of Northampton on 1 May 1994.

1. C. Brusselmans, 'Key faith communities: family, parish, school' (article looking to the forthcoming Roman Synod on Catechesis), *National Catholic Reporter* (12 August 1977).
2. J. Audinet, 'Catechesis: the church building the church in a given culture', *Our Apostolate* (Sydney), vol. 24, no. 3 (1976).
3. F. H. Drinkwater, editorial, *The Sower*, no. 1 (June 1919).
4. 1977 Synod, 'Message to the People of God', *Briefing*, vol. 7, no. 32 (29 October 1977).
5. General Conclusions of Medellín International Study Week, p. 69, in M. Warren (ed.), *Sourcebook for Modern Catechetics* (Winona, MN: St Mary's Press, 1983).
6. 'Living and Sharing Our Faith', the National Project of Catechesis and Religious Education, was begun in the 1980s as an initiative of the Bishops' Conference of England and Wales. The National Project, comprising several books and initiatives, is a response to the vision of a developing church which touches people of every age-group in homes, schools and parishes.
7. Pope Pius X, *Acerbo Nimis*: ET as 'The teaching of catechism', *The Tablet* (29 April 1905).
8. F. H. Drinkwater, 'On the making of catechisms', *Downside Review*, no. 256 (Spring 1956), p. 130.
9. *Catechism of the Catholic Church* (London: Geoffrey Chapman, 1994).
10. B. Wicker, 'A theology of the gramophone', *The Tablet* (20 September 1986).
11. A. Nebreda, *Kerygma in Crisis?* (Chicago: Loyola University Press, 1965), pp. viii–ix.
12. See 'Focus on education for Christian living' in C. Jamison, D. Lundy and L. Poole, *To Live Is To Change: A Way of Reading Vatican II* (London: Rejoice Publications, 1994).
13. B. Marthaler, 'The modern catechetical movement in Roman Catholicism', *Religious Education*, 73 (1978).
14. E. Schillebeeckx, *The Understanding of Faith* (London: Sheed and Ward, 1974), p. xi (language adapted).
15. F. H. Drinkwater, 'De Catechizandibus Parvulis' (1933), reprinted in *Educational Essays* (London: Burns and Oates, 1951), p. 340.
16. John Baptist de La Salle, 'Meditation on St Anne' in *Meditations* (ET; London: Waldegrave, 1953), p. 575.
17. Pope Paul VI, *Evangelii Nuntiandi*: ET as 'Evangelisation today', *Doctrine and Life* (March–April 1977), p. 39.
18. Pope John Paul II, *Christifideles Laici* (London: CTS, 1989), p. 17.
19. Marthaler, op. cit.
20. Useful studies of the twentieth-century French catechetical movement are G. Adler and G. Vogeleisen, *Un siècle de catéchèse en France, 1893–1980* (Paris: Beauchesne, 1981), and Mary Coke, *Le Mouvement Catéchétique* (Paris: Centurion, 1988).
21. James Parker, 'The mother of Christian Initiation', *Commonweal* (31 January 1992).
22. H. J. Richards and P. de Rosa, preface to Gabriel Moran, *God Still Speaks* (London: Burns and Oates, 1967), p. 11.

23. Congregation for Catholic Education, *The Religious Dimension of Education in a Catholic School* (London: CTS, 1988), paragraph 7.

24. Vatican II, *Gaudium et Spes*, sections 4–10: ET in N. Tanner SJ (ed.), *Decrees of the Ecumenical Councils*, vol. 2 (Washington, DC: Georgetown University Press/London: Sheed and Ward, 1990), p. 1074.

25. *New Religious Movements: A Challenge to the Church* (London: Catholic Truth Society, 1986).

26. Ibid., p. 11.

27. F. von Hügel, *The Mystical Element of Religion as Studied in St Catherine of Genoa and Her Friends* (London, 1908), 1923.

28. Evelyn Woodward, *Poets, Prophets and Pragmatists* (Blackburn, Victoria: Collins Dove, 1987), p. 25.

29. F. H. Drinkwater, 'Conscience emergent', *New Blackfriars* (February 1966), reprinted in *The Secret Name* (Leominster: Fowler Wright, 1986), p. 201.

30. Brusselmans, op. cit.

Mystagogy: a model for sacramental catechesis

6

CATHERINE DOOLEY OP

IN THE PAST DECADE there has been a search for an alternative to the classroom model of catechesis/religious education which has been dominant since the Reformation. Even though curriculum-based religious education has changed significantly from a focus on instruction to an integrated approach that incorporates formation of community, dedication to service, prayer, worship, and doctrine, nevertheless there continues to be discussion about a sacramental preparation that would be more formative of a sacramental spirituality. The desire for a new paradigm receives impetus from the restoration of the Rite of Christian Initiation of Adults. Dr Christiane Brusselmans made a bold beginning by incorporating many of the principles of the RCIA into parish programmes for first penance and Eucharist. In a conversation Christiane said that a future direction was to implement more fully and completely the period of mystagogy as integral to initiation. In Christiane's memory I would like to explore the nature and foundational principles of mystagogy and offer a process for its implementation in order to continue the conversation.

NATURE OF MYSTAGOGY

The Rite of Christian Initiation of Adults describes mystagogy or post-baptismal catechesis:

> a time for the community and the neophytes together to grow in deepening their grasp of the paschal mystery and in making it part of

their lives through meditation on the Gospel, sharing in the eucharist and doing the works of charity. (RCIA 234)

This contemporary understanding of mystagogy recognizes that all life experience is capable of manifesting God; the purpose of mystagogy is to identify and appropriate God's loving presence which already exists in the lives of the community and the neophytes. Contemporary mystagogy receives its inspiration from the postbaptismal catechesis of the fourth and fifth centuries where 'mystagogy' was through the homilies given during Easter week following the celebration of the rites of initiation at the Easter Vigil. Cyril of Jerusalem provides the rationale for this catechesis:

> . . . since seeing is far more persuasive than hearing, I delayed until the present occasion knowing that I would find you more open to the influence of my words out of your personal experience . . .[1]

The 'text' of the homily then is 'the experience of the liturgical actions that constitute sacramental celebrations',[2] that is, both the initiation rites and the reflection upon the rites in terms of one's life are the elements of mystagogy. The mystagogue suggests, clarifies and extends the meaning of sacramental initiation in order to bring the neophytes to a deeper participation and to prepare them to live a life of faithfulness to Christ.

The mystagogical homilies are characterized by certain interlocking components: biblical stories and images as foundational to liturgical celebration; liturgical feasts and/or seasons as a key to interpretation; and symbolic liturgical action as powerful communication. The purpose was to lead not only to a deeper appreciation of the liturgical celebration by which the neophyte names, appropriates and celebrates the awesome mystery of God's love but to adopting a sacramental vision of life by which one is able to look at one's own life through the eyes of faith and discover an inner and deeper meaning in the ordinary.

The methodology was to appeal continually to a biblical typology, which, in interrelating the two Testaments, was one of the primary means of interpreting Scripture in the patristic period. 'This method does not give priority to the New Testament over the Old or the Old over the New; it requires both to be continually referred each to the other.'[3] The assumption is that in the Bible there is a consistency in the pattern of God's saving action in both Testaments so the events, persons and realities of the Old Testament are 'types' or 'images' that give meaning to or are antecedents of events, persons, and realities in the New Testament. It is the juxtaposing of images, the relationship between them that gives insight into the mystery. Typology therefore is the search for correspondences and relationships within the framework of historical revelation.

Whatever scholars may think of typology today as a method of exegesis, it had a twofold importance in the patristic period. It stretched the imagination of the hearers by presenting many images that gave insight into the mystery and provided a biblical foundation for participation in the liturgical rites. The use of typology placed the present celebration within the context of the whole of the history of salvation: the bread of the Eucharist was compared with the manna in the desert; baptism is prefigured in the crossing of the Red Sea, in the flood, in the healing of the paralytic in the pool of Bethsaida, so that the neophyte might recognize the unity of God's word and work. For the mystagogues, the events in the story of salvation not only revealed God's presence in the past but that presence is expressed and effected now in the sacramental life as it is lived out in the community's everyday life.

FOUNDATIONAL PRINCIPLES OF MYSTAGOGY

The contemporary rite of initiation claims this biblical/liturgical perspective of the early mystagogues as the foundational principles for a renewed sacramental catechesis or mystagogy:

(1) *Interrelationship of the sacraments*

The RCIA restores the original order and unity of the sacraments of initiation – baptism, confirmation and Eucharist. Each of these sacraments identifies the individual as sharer in the paschal mystery and member of the Body of Christ. The *Ordo* names baptism and Eucharist as fundamental sacraments and the other sacraments are understood in relationship to them. Questions about confirmation, penance or anointing are baptismal questions and questions about marriage and orders are eucharistic questions.[4] The sacraments are not seven discrete linear events that parallel human growth but rather they draw their meaning from and return to the fundamental sacraments.

(2) *The word of God is integral to liturgical celebration*

The documents of Vatican II re-established the use of Scripture in every celebration of the liturgy. The Constitution on the Sacred Liturgy (CSL 7) of Vatican II reminds us that when the word is proclaimed, it is God who speaks to us. This word is living and active through the power of the Holy Spirit and expresses God's love that never fails in its effectiveness towards us (InLM 4[5]). In the hearing of God's word the Church is built up and grows. Whenever the Church, gathered by the Holy Spirit for liturgical celebration, announces and proclaims the word of God, it has the experience of being a new people in whom the covenant made in the past is fulfilled (InLM 7).

(3) Symbols and symbolic actions are the language of faith

Symbols and symbolic actions are the ways in which the presence of Christ and his mystery is manifest to the worshipping community and the way in which the community's response to God's initiative is made evident. The liturgical action, which revolves around the central symbols of gathering the assembly, proclaiming of the word, immersing in water, sharing of bread and wine, anointing with oil, laying on of hands, aims to enable the people of God to experience the mystery of God and to lead lives of Christian discipleship. These central symbols belong to the very nature of the sacraments, enabling the believer to move from the visible to the invisible, that is, from what is seen and experienced to interpretation or meaning. Symbolic language is intuitive, non-verbal and non-discursive; it touches the whole person. In view of the prevailing culture's emphasis on the rational, it is important to underline a more total approach to the human person 'by opening up and developing the non-rational elements of liturgical celebration: the concerns for feelings of conversion, support, joy, repentance, trust, love, memory, movement, gesture, wonder'.[6] The symbols communicate not by removing ambiguity but by flooding the senses with it. The non-verbal and the experiential nature of the rites has the power to form and to transform the human person.

(4) Liturgy is related to life

Life is a continuing process and the sacraments are privileged moments within that process. Sacraments are not restricted to the moment of celebration but include all the efforts toward conversion that take place before and after the liturgy as well as the actual celebration. Not only do the sacraments express the life of the Christian but they call Christians to live out day by day the mystery of faith which they have just celebrated. The liturgy offers a vision of justice, peace, unity and reconciliation still to be attained, not only among Christians but among the whole human family.

(5) The assembly has a right and an obligation to full, active and conscious participation in the liturgy

The RCIA presumes the full, active and conscious participation of the community in the initiation process and event. The ecclesiology of the *Ordo* names the assembly as the Spirit-filled Body of Christ. Just as Christ is the visible manifestation and tangible presence of God so too the Church is the sacrament of Christ in history until he comes again. Christ is present in and through this assembly, just as he is present in the presiding minister, in the word proclaimed, and indeed substantially and unceasingly in the eucharistic bread and wine (CSL 7). This one presence of Christ manifested in different modes is foundational to a sacramental vision.

The ecclesial dimension of the Rite is not only evidenced in the specific ministries – sponsor, godparent, catechist, ordained minister – but it is through the prayer, example and involvement of the whole Church that the catechumen comes to faith.

This communal perspective is also seen in the understanding that sacraments are sacraments of faith, which is the faith not only of the individual but of the Church as a whole. It is in and through the Church's faith – the faith that has come to us from the apostles, the faith of the local church, and the faith of the domestic church[7] – that the individual comes to personal faith.

(6) Catechesis is an integrated process of formation

Catechesis includes building up the community, integrating scriptural and doctrinal instruction into reflection on experience, leading to private and liturgical prayer and motivating the acts of justice. Catechesis is an ongoing process, and an awareness of the formative nature of ritual is a constitutive element of that process.[8] The *Catechism of the Catholic Church* states that the liturgy is 'the privileged place for catechizing the People of God' (no. 1074) and calls for a liturgical catechesis, which 'aims to initiate people into the mystery of Christ (it is "mystagogy") by proceeding from the visible to the invisible, from the sign to the thing signified, from the "sacraments" to the "mysteries"' (no. 1075).

(7) The sacraments call us to commitment

To say that the Church is the sacrament of Christ is also to state the Church's identity and mission. When the Church gathered in assembly carries out this ministry and mission through its ritual actions, it makes present and effectively continues the saving work of Christ. *The Catechism of the Catholic Church* states that the Eucharist commits us to the poor (no. 1397). In the Christian tradition, the very participation in the Eucharist necessarily involves action for justice. If in truth we repeat the actions of Jesus at the Supper and share the body and blood of Christ given up for us, then the 'do this' in the memory of Jesus can only mean attention to the very real needs of our world today.

(8) The liturgical year expresses and shapes Christian identity

Sunday is *the* day for Christians to gather for worship. This is attested to in the second century by Justin Martyr[9] and reaffirmed in the present time as a tradition handed down from the apostles. In the course of the year the whole mystery of Christ is recalled and the culmination of the church year is the Easter triduum of the passion and resurrection of Christ. All of the Sundays, seasons and feasts of the year express a different aspect of the paschal mystery. The penitential and baptismal character of Lent, the vigilance and expectation of Advent, the beginning of the paschal mystery manifested in the birth, epiphany and baptism of Jesus of the Christmas season, and accounts of Jesus' ministry and the celebration of the paschal mystery in all of its aspects in Ordinary time shape and express Catholic identity as well as promoting formation and participation in the life of the Church.[10]

PROCESS FOR IMPLEMENTATION

The mystagogy of the early Church offers a model for contemporary sacramental catechesis with its biblical/liturgical orientation and its pattern of a catechesis for the liturgy, participation in and celebration of the rites and a post-baptismal reflection (mystagogy) that leads to action. These phases are integrated and interlocking aspects of a single process.

Catechesis for the liturgy

Liturgical catechesis begins first with the assembly who are celebrating, with the text and readings of the rite itself and the feasts and seasons of the liturgical year. The theology of the rite and the principles of catechesis are found in the Introduction (*praenotanda*) of the rite. Questions such as these may be helpful to guide the catechist's preparation:

A. Who is the parish community into whom the candidates will be initiated?
   1. What is the age, ability, culture, vocation of the participants?
   2. What are some major cultural symbols important to this group of people?
   3. What social/political/economic factors are affecting the people of this area?
B. Introduction to the rite and to the texts of the rite
   1. Principles of catechesis
      (a) What are the key principles for catechesis found in the Introduction?
      (b) How does this sacrament relate to baptism/Eucharist?
      (c) What is the purpose of the rite according to the Introduction?
      (d) What is the role of the community in this rite?
      (e) What is the appropriate time and place for the celebration?
   2. What images are used to describe the sacrament/rite in the Introduction to the rite and in the prayer texts of the rite?
      (a) What are the symbolic actions (e.g. sign of the cross) and elements (e.g. water, oil) used in the rite?
      (b) Why are these actions/elements used in this rite? (historical and doctrinal background)
      (c) What are the human experiences that are being expressed in the rite?
C. Lectionary/rite study
   1. What Scripture texts are suggested for the rite?
      (a) What images are central in the Scripture readings and in the prayers of the rite?
      (b) How do these images relate to the symbols/symbolic actions of the rite?
      (c) How do these images relate to the life of the community? (See A above.)
   2. What biblical background is necessary in order to have greater appreciation of the readings?
   3. What idea of God, Jesus, and Holy Spirit do the readings give to us? What idea of the human person? community?

D. Liturgical season
   1. What liturgical season is being celebrated?
   2. How do the themes of the season relate to the readings? How do they relate to the prayers and text of the rite?
   3. What are appropriate music selections correlating the season/feast and the ritual?

For example, in the rite of becoming a catechumen, the rite is the starting point. The suggested readings, the prayers and the actions offer a number of images that form the basis of the catechesis: journey, identification by name, call and response, faith of the Church, being marked by the cross or the power of the word. The purpose here is not to explain the rite but to explore the various images in their scriptural, historical and liturgical aspects as well as in the candidate's own experience in order to build up a whole vocabulary of associations that the candidate can bring to the celebration as a means of interpretation. In the focus on identification by name, questions such as these could be used:

What positive or negative importance do names have for the identity of an individual or a community?
When have you been aware of the power of names or of naming?
What are some of the reasons parents choose a particular name for their child?
Why were you given your name?

Explore the significance of the names or naming in the Scriptures using passages such as these: Genesis 2:19–20; 17:2–8, 15–16; Matthew 1:21, 16:16. It will become clear to the candidates that name is both identity and call/response.

Next consider the meaning of name within the rite of acceptance into the order of catechumens. The first question asked of the candidate is: 'What is your name?' In the rite the group is first addressed as candidates and then as catechumens.

What is the significance of the change of name from candidate to catechumen?
What is the relationship of the change of name to the signing with the cross?
What is the relationship of the change of name to the change of name within the Scriptures?

If each of the central themes were explored from the aspects of experience, Scripture and ritual, it would seem that the catechumens would have a wealth of images with which to more fully enter into the celebration of the rite.

Catechesis through the liturgy

The celebration of the rite and mystagogy are all of a piece. Liturgy fosters and expresses Catholic Christian identity. It shapes the attitudes, values and way of looking at life, often without much real awareness on our part. In the liturgy, the Church remembers all God's saving actions in history which culminated in the death and resurrection of Jesus Christ.

> But the paschal event, which occurred only once in history, is contemporary with each moment of our own lives, . . . we do the remembering, but the reality remembered is no longer in the past but is here: the Church's memory becomes a presence.[11]

The liturgy is not a way in which we enter into the mystery of Christ. It is the mystery. Moreover, ritual not only brings together those who are celebrating but unites us with those who have gone before and those who are yet to come. The ritual not only expresses the present but calls us to transformation. We are always in the position of the already and the not yet. The rites offer a critique of our life as individuals and as a community because they hold out a vision of what it means to be Christian.

Mystagogy or catechesis from the sacrament

Again the catechist needs to ask a series of questions that are grouped around the personal experience in relationship to the rite.

A. Personal experience
  1. What was the individual's experience of the rite?
  2. What were commonalities in the experience of the group?
  3. What biblical images were evident to the participants? In what other readings do we find these same images? What is the relationship?
  4. How do the prayers and readings relate to the participant's life experience?
  5. What meaning did the symbolic actions have for the participant?

B. Action
   1. How do the readings/prayers/rite call one to conversion?
   2. Is there a concrete step/action that each needs to take? that they
      need to do as a community?

The questions indicate a progression: from reflection on the community's experience of the liturgical actions, which may include personal response, an explanation of doctrine, or an historical perspective; to reflection on the Scripture as it is shaped by the liturgical season; to an exploration of the ethical consequences: what change does it demand in the person/community's outlook/actions?

The Second Sunday of Easter (Cycle A) may be used as an example of a catechesis with neophytes. In the early Church the newly baptized who wore their baptismal garments during the week following Easter put them aside on this day.[12] The lectionary readings for the day focus on various aspects of faith. The first reading (Acts 2:42–47) tells us that those who believed shared all things in common and by their assent to the gospel accepted responsibility for one another and were themselves transformed. The second reading (1 Peter 1:3–9) speaks of the faith that guards the baptized with God's power, of the faith that needs to be tried in order to be purified, of the faith that enables believers to love Christ Jesus even though they have never seen him, and finally the goal of faith: salvation. The gospel (John 20:19–31) is the account of the so-called doubting Thomas whose story is recorded so that we all might believe even though we have not seen.

The newly baptized have heard these readings and are asked to think about Thomas's response when he was told that the disciples had seen Jesus and then when Jesus appeared to him. In talking about Thomas's story, people often naturally reveal their own stories.

Ask the group to think back to the beginning of their process of initiation when they were asked: 'What do you ask of God's Church?' and they replied 'faith'. Then they were asked: 'What does faith offer you?' and the answer was 'eternal life'. Pray with them the opening prayer from the Rite of Acceptance that ends:

> This is the way of faith along which Christ will lead you in love toward eternal life. Are you prepared to begin this journey today under the guidance of Christ?

Reflect with the neophytes on how they understood the way of faith at the beginning of their journey and how God, though unseen, was revealed to them. How did their understanding of faith then differ from their understanding now as they professed their faith in baptism?

A refrain throughout the gospel is 'Peace be with you'. The meaning of the greeting of peace is an obvious liturgical action upon which to reflect in the light of the gospel.

CONCLUSION

Baptismal identity expressed and renewed in the Eucharist forms Christians throughout their lives. For that reason mystagogy is not limited to the Sundays after Easter but is a continuing process of reflection taking place within the midst of the community.[13] Mystagogy engages the imagination. It evokes rather than explains. It enlightens rather than defines. Mystagogy brings together personal story and the images of the Scripture with the actions and relationships of the liturgy. It fosters a sacramental vision that gives us a new way to name and to know God.

NOTES

1. F. L. Cross (ed.), *St Cyril of Jerusalem's Lectures on the Christian Sacraments* (Crestwood, NY: St Vladimir's Seminary Press, 1977), p. 53.

2. Samuel E. Torvend, 'Preaching the liturgy: a social mystagogy' in Regina Siegfried and Edward Ruane (eds), *In the Company of Preachers* (Collegeville, MN: The Liturgical Press, 1993), p. 61.

3. Enrico Mazza, *Mystagogy* (New York: Pueblo Publishing, 1989), pp. 10–11.

4. Aidan Kavanagh, 'Theological principles for sacramental catechesis', *Living Light* 23/4 (June 1987), p. 317.

5. InLM = *Introduction to the Lectionary for Mass* (New York: Catholic Book Publishing Co., 1970).

6. US Bishops' Committee on the Liturgy (BCL), *Environment and Art in Catholic Worship* (EAW), 35: in *The Liturgy Documents* (Chicago: Liturgy Training Publications, 1991), p. 325.

7. The *Catechism of the Catholic Church* (no. 1666) states that the Christian home is the place where children receive the first proclamation of the faith. For this reason, the family home is rightly called the 'domestic church', a community of grace and prayer, a school of human virtues and of Christian charity.

8. In the past decade the discussion has shifted more and more to the meaning of liturgical catechesis, its aim, content and methodology. The Liturgy of the Word with children

apart from the Sunday assembly and lectionary catechesis have been factors in this discussion.

9. Justin Martyr, *First Apology*, chapters 66–67, cited in Johannes Emminghaus, *The Eucharist* (Collegeville, MN: Liturgical Press, 1988), pp. 35–6.

10. For a brief helpful introduction to the liturgical year, see nos 25–48 of the Introduction to the *Lectionary for Masses with Children* (Washington, DC: US Bishops' Committee on the Liturgy, 1993).

11. Jean Corbon, *The Wellspring of Worship* (New York: Paulist Press, 1988), pp. 5–6.

12. See J. D. C. Fisher for sources on the wearing of the white robe for the week called the *dies albae*: *Christian Initiation: Baptism in the Medieval West* (London: SPCK, 1965), p. 65.

13. Mystagogy as continuing process is treated in Stefan Knobloch and Herbert Haslinger (eds), *Mystagogische Seelsorge: Eine lebensgeschichtlich orientierte Pastoral* (Mainz: Matthias-Grunewald, 1991).

Mixed signals

priestly identity and priestly spirituality since Vatican II

KENAN B. OSBORNE OFM

THE SPIRITUALITY OF THE PRIEST has been a theme of considerable discussion, during both the Second Vatican Council and the entire period after it. This has occurred for many reasons, but the deepest reason of all seems to be the re-identification or redefinition of a priest which is found in the Vatican documents themselves. Deliberately, the conciliar bishops moved away from the scholastic understanding of priesthood, and presented their material on the ordained priest through the priestliness of Jesus, which, as the bishops said, involved the *tria munera*: a ministry of preaching/teaching, a ministry of sanctifying and a ministry of leadership (prophet, priest, king).[1] Through such changes in the very meaning and identity of priestly ministry, a rethinking of priestly spirituality became imperative.

OFFICIAL STATEMENTS ON PRIESTLY SPIRITUALITY

Let us consider, at this first stage of our investigation, some of the key ecclesiastical documents which have focused on the issue of priestly spirituality. Foremost among them for our times is the decree from Vatican II on the ministry and life of priests, *Presbyterorum Ordinis* (1965).

Presbyterorum Ordinis

It is well known that the bishops at Vatican II had fundamental difficulties with the various preliminary drafts of this decree, which eventually led to the final text as we know it today. The bishops were divided on a major issue: should a discussion on the ministry of a priest be treated first, or should a discussion on the spiritual life of a priest be first? The bishops clearly saw that if the ministry of a priest were treated first, then ministry itself would govern the ways in which priestly spirituality would be presented, and this, in the eyes of some bishops, would make both priestly identity and priestly spirituality more functional than 'ontological'. On the other hand, if priestly life and priestly spirituality were treated first, then priestly ministry would be seen as flowing directly from one's life and one's spirituality.[2]

As we know now, priestly ministry eventually became the first theme treated, and the theme of priestly life was formulated on the basis of priestly ministry. Accordingly, in the document the office of priesthood is viewed primarily in terms of its function and not of its status, and priestly life, including priestly spirituality, is defined and stamped by priestly ministry, by priestly function, and by priestly mission. At least this is the main thrust of Presbyterorum Ordinis, although the opposite view can be found, but only here and there, in the document itself. Since this document, like all the Vatican II documents, was at times clearly a compromise document, statements had to be inserted here and there which would satisfy opposing views. During the lengthy preliminary discussions on this particular document, many bishops urged a number of textual alterations, most strongly in the section of the document which addressed the issue of priestly holiness, that is, nos 12 to 16. The insistence and urgency behind many of these alterations indicated that this theme, priestly holiness, was one of the most sensitive themes of the entire issue of priestly ministry and life.[3]

The following characteristics of priestly spirituality emerge from the final and approved text of Presbyterorum Ordinis:

1. Priestly ministry and priestly spirituality are fundamentally Christo-centric: there is a special union between the ordained priest and Jesus, the High Priest.[4]
2. Priestly ministry and priestly spirituality are, as a result, united to the ministry and mission of Jesus, which is continued in the mission and

ministry of the Church. God has 'set' certain people 'apart' for this mission and ministry.[5]

3. Priestly consecration is related to baptismal consecration, but on this matter the decree rather one-sidedly stresses in its description of consecration a single issue: the call to perfection. The final wording of this particular paragraph has caused no little post-conciliar discussion.[6]

4. Priestly perfection is related specifically to the *tria munera*, in which the ministry to the word of God is given primacy of place, that is, preaching is mentioned as the first ministry of every priest. Secondly, the priest involves himself in a ministry of sanctification. Thirdly, a priest involves himself in a ministry of leadership and pastoral care.[7]

5. Priestly perfection, the document notes, can be threatened by the volume of ministerial work, and therefore a priest must give adequate attention to personal growth of the 'interior life'. Mention is made at this juncture of some specific religious practices which a priest should engage in on a regular basis, namely, the recitation of the breviary, the rosary, meditation.[8]

6. Priestly spirituality is presented in even more detail under the umbrella of the evangelical counsels. Obedience is enumerated first, then celibacy, and lastly poverty. The majority of bishops had made a determined effort not to make mini-monks out of presbyters, but the threefold schematic – obedience, chastity and poverty – prevailed. In many ways, this was occasioned by the intervention of Paul VI, which disallowed any conciliar discussion on the matter of priestly celibacy.[9]

These six issues offer the main characteristics of priestly spirituality which this document offers to us. One can, however, quite legitimately ask: is this an adequate framework for priestly spirituality today? What are its strong points and what are its weaknesses?

Without entering into a major response to such questions, one could note that the idea of the *tria munera* itself might not be adequate for either Christology or ecclesiology. In the ecumenical discussions with certain Eastern churches, the need for the theology of icon has been strongly suggested, and this theology of icon would then play a role in the understanding and ministry of the priest as well. The priest is an icon of Jesus who is an icon of God. Second, one might note that the relationship of ordained priesthood to baptism/Eucharist is only mentioned in this section of the document but not developed in any profound way, in spite of the emphasis on the word *Christifidelis* which is found in many of the other documents of Vatican II, most notably in the Council's major document, *Lumen Gentium*. What *Lumen Gentium* states and what *Presbyterorum Ordinis* states are, at times, not all that compatible.[10] Third, one might note that the spirituality of *Presbyterorum Ordinis* reverts once again to the monastic framework of the 'evangelical counsels', a term supposedly connoting something different than the term 'three vows', but which nonetheless only thinly veils the spirituality of a vowed life, making the priest once again into a mini-monk.

As One Who Serves

Secondly, one might consider the document from the National Conference of the Bishops of the United States: *As One Who Serves*, which appeared in 1977.[11] In general, this is an excellent document, but only in the final section of the document, namely in the section which is entitled 'Growth in Christ', is the spirituality of the priesthood dealt with in any focused way.[12] In these few pages, the emphasis is centred exclusively on prayer: various kinds of prayer, reception of the sacrament of reconciliation, and the celebration of the Eucharist.

In many ways, however, this final brief section does make an attempt to sum up several issues on priestly identity and priestly life which are found throughout this same document. Of singular importance for our purposes in this essay is the description of priestly ministry found in the section entitled 'Nature of priestly ministry'.[13] At this juncture, the document indicates that in several statements from the Second Vatican Council priestly ministry is described in its corporate character.

> This service of ministry (diakonia) has a corporate character. For all those made one by Baptism into Christ thereby share in his ministry. Ministry, then, is the vocation, privilege, and responsibility of all members of the Church ... The whole Church is the primary recipient of Christ's mission, and each individual from Pope through layperson can operate only in community with the whole Church and as part of the whole body. 'The brotherhood and equality of all members takes precedence over all later distinctions and persists in them.' In this sense the People of God as a whole enjoy a basic collegiality, a common servanthood.[14]

The American bishops then proceed to discuss the corporate relationship between bishop and priest. They point out that there were in the Council's many references to the relationship of bishop and priest two fairly definite lines of thought. The first is stated as follows:

> Priests are assistants to the bishop, dependent on him, act in his name, have priesthood in a limited degree, make the bishop present, take on his duties and concerns, are sons to the bishop as father. All these references stress either the apartness of the bishop or a paternal nearness, neither of which features serves to emphasize a common servanthood and partnership.[15]

The American bishops then point out that in the same Vatican II reference areas there was indicated another more clearly fraternal relationship:

> Priests are fellow-workers, co-workers, friends; they constitute one priesthood with their bishop, participate in and exercise with their bishop the one priesthood of Christ. These references speak to a partnership and brotherly orientation, one that seems to go beyond the differentiation of roles and that sets common discipleship and collegial service as prior objectives ... This kind of relationship of bishops with priests stresses their essential unity of mission.[16]

As One Who Serves favours the latter approach, and then asks: what makes the priest special within the Church of God? The document answers in a way well known to many:

> The priest, then, officially personifies the self-understanding and mission of the Church. It is not his functions as such that fully reveal his nature, for the functions can change or become separate ministries performed by others.[17]

What an interesting statement, since this separation of function from the person of the priest raises the issue as regards such ministries as the celebration of Mass: could this ministry become a separate ministry performed by others? Or could the ministry of forgiving sins in the sacrament of reconciliation be separated and then performed by others?

The form of priestly ministry, the document continues, has seen many historical variations, which differ one from the other in considerable measure. This is abundantly true, but is there, then, an abiding element in priestly ministry? The answer which the document gives is as follows:

> The abiding element in the priestly ministry is rooted in the abiding character of the Church. The Church will always have its radical need for a priestly ministry to assume and make present that complex of tasks and functions which are necessary for this community of faith, hope and love.[18]

Such a statement does not quite make sense, since the document reverts immediately back to tasks and functions, even though it had attempted to move away from tasks and functions. In all of this, one moves from 'function to identity' or from 'identity to function'. The ambiguity which exhibits itself at times in *As One Who Serves* is evidence of the post-conciliar struggle to work through the major changes in the very understanding of a priest which the documents of Vatican II engendered.

The Formation of Priests in Circumstances of the Present Day

One should also consider the 1990 synodal working document on the *Formation of Priests in Circumstances of the Present Day*, which deals almost exclusively with the piety of priestly candidates, and therefore in the long run with the piety of a priest.[19] The spirituality offered in this document is basically personal, ethical and private, not ministerial, social and public. The spirituality in the document, in a general way, but not as clearly as one might hope, follows some of the guidelines from the Vatican II documents,[20] but the document in general is clearly a reversion to a more privatized and devotional form of spirituality.

Paragraph no. 14, in my view, is the central statement of the document, but the ideas within it are not used in either an operative or a centralizing way. We read:

> All priests then are called to mission. Even if some are specially prepared for certain situations and specific mission tasks in the Church, all are bound to serve the work of mission as a result of their ordination. Their primary function is in effect 'to announce the gospel of God to all' and to 'spread the faith'; therefore, they must

feel the need to devote themselves to 'sharing with all the truth of the gospel'.[21]

A key idea in the above passage is: the primary function of priests is to be messengers of the Gospel. This idea, if indeed it is meant to be primary, should have been given primacy of place in the document: a primacy of place from which the entire document unfolds. Otherwise, it is foolish to call this the primary function of the priest and not contextualize it in its role of primacy. Had it been given a primacy of place, which would have to a great degree unified the document, then two themes would stand out in a most special way:

1. The primary function, as stated in no. 14, requires that priestly spirituality be Gospel spirituality.
2. The primary function, as stated in no. 14, demands that a priestly candidate be academically and spiritually trained for the task of mission.

The first point is very apropos to our theme: every candidate for the priesthood who is not profoundly and spiritually anxious and eager to bring the Gospel to others should be considered far from the mark of readiness for ordination. Moreover, any priest who is not anxious and eager to bring the Gospel to others is clearly far from the mark of a true priest. Priestly spirituality is pastoral spirituality. Priests who are too timid or too uninterested to leave either the monastery or the rectory and evangelize the world in which they find themselves are by no means the kind of priest the Church leadership wishes to form today. Had no. 14 been taken seriously by the synod, then there would have been a primacy of place given to an evangelizing spirituality. Unfortunately, the document does not carry through on what it itself says is the primary function of the priest.

The second point also has reference to our theme, since both the academic training and spiritual training move in a concerted direction: to be a messenger of the Gospel. The theology which a priest learns and puts into practice must be a pastoral theology; the spirituality which accompanies this academic formation must be a pastoral spirituality.

Other documents could be added to this list, but these indicate quite clearly that spirituality of the priesthood is a much discussed topic today, and also that the spirituality of the priesthood, even when presented by official Church statements, is not developed in a totally uniform way. This non-uniformity of description from such top-level Church offices cannot but leave us today with many questions: What can we make of this theme of priestly spirituality? Why are we hearing 'mixed signals' on this issue? How can we envision its future?

PRIESTLY IDENTITY

Robert Schwartz notes in his book *Servant Leaders of the People of God* that 'the self-understanding of priests establishes their basic spiritual identity'.[22] Self-understanding is the source of one's spirituality. This identity, he states, has threefold dimension, and therefore there is a threefold source of priestly spirituality. The first is the foundation of one's human dimension and one's self-identity as a human being, and this identity is a major source of priestly spirituality. The second is the foundation of one's Christian dimension and one's Christian identity which priests have in common with all baptized/eucharistic Christians, and this Christian identity is a major source of priestly spirituality. The third is the distinctive identity of priests as 'participants in Christ, the servant-head of the church'.[23] This comes from the sacrament of order, whereby a priest is consecrated to act publicly in the person of Christ *vis-à-vis* the ecclesial community and as a representative of the bishop.

The direction that Schwartz takes here is extremely helpful for a contemporary understanding of priestly identity and spirituality. Spirituality is based on one's identity, and this is a major insight. If one does not analyse one's self-identity and nourish it, one can never develop a strong spirituality. I believe that there is a fourth root to one's identity, namely culture, and so priestly spirituality rests on a fourfold, not a threefold basis.[24]

The identity of being human

Over the centuries the philosophers and theologians have tried again and again to 'define' what it means to be a human person. The mystery of human life has been elusive. Very powerful and helpful descriptions of the human person can be found in Plato and Aristotle, in Confucius and Mencius, in Augustine and Boethius, in Thomas Aquinas and John Duns

Scotus. More recently, we have equally brilliant descriptions in the writings of Descartes, Kant, Hegel, Marx, Heidegger, Ricoeur. Many other names could easily be added to this list. Still, the mystery of human life remains precisely what the phrase indicates: a mystery. Perhaps, no final definition or description will ever be developed.

When we ask the opposite question: when do we find ourselves feeling dehumanized? the answers vary as well. More often than not, however, the answer tends towards the area of loneliness. When we feel that no one cares, no one listens, no one loves us, it is then that we think murky thoughts of despair, even suicide. Human life seems to have no further meaning for us.

In many lectures and discussions, I have suggested to priests, as I speak of the mystery of human identity, that they take a small piece of paper and on one side write down the names of those people who truly love them. On the opposite side of the small piece of paper, they are asked to write down the names of those people whom they themselves truly love. People have many friends and acquaintances, but generally those whom we love and those who love us are a special few. If a priest has no names on either side of the small piece of paper, his spiritual problems are not from his priesthood nor from his Christian faith, but from his humanity. Often priests who are isolated and socially aloof will feel that their spiritual life is amiss and look to their priestliness for a solution or they will look to their prayer and faith life for a resolution. The cause rests in neither of these areas; it rests in the shrivelled humanity of the priest involved. Everyone, celibate or married, needs to love someone and to let someone love him/her. Without strong and loving relationships our human identity withers.

Christian identity

Time and again, calling something 'Christian' does not rouse a priest to action; but calling something 'priestly' often does cause a priest to act. When one analyses this situation, one realizes that for some priests the 'Christian' element is secondary, while the 'priestly' element is primary. However, a question arises: is one not first of all and basically Christian? Is not one's baptism/Eucharist more important and more fundamental than the sacrament of order? Without baptism and Eucharist, without Church, without Jesus, a Christian priest has no meaning whatsoever. In this scenario, one asks priests: do you really believe in Jesus, in the Church, in the communion of baptized Christians, in the people of God? Or do you only believe in priestly things? Where is the depth of your faith?

Again, there are priests who have become 'career priests'. They remain in the priesthood even though their faith is no longer a major power in their life. They fulfil their duties and functions, but the heart is not there. When their spirituality begins to fall apart, it is not priesthood which is causing the destruction, it is, rather, the lack of faith.

Cultural identity

With the increased sensitivity to a multi-cultural world, and with an increased awareness of the need for inculturation and acculturation, one is aware that culture plays a central role in one's personal identity. One cannot simply take a Euro-American idea of priest and ask that African-cultured people, or Hispanic-cultured people or Asian-cultured people – each with their own multi-cultural differences – become basically and fundamentally Euro-American priests, who simply speak a different language. When culture is suppressed, identity is deeply injured. One must rethink priest from a variety of African-cultured positions, from a variety of Hispanic-cultured situations, from a variety of Asian-cultured histories. This cultural identification will evidence itself, as a result, in some form of African-cultured spirituality, some form of Hispanic-cultured spirituality and some form of Asian-cultured spirituality. In these various cultures, one will not find a priest who reflects a basically Euro-American spirituality.

It is not simply a question of inculturating the idea of priest within a variety of cultures. Rather, there is a larger question: namely, the entire understanding of Christian community and Christian ministry needs to be thought through from the basic and foundational building-blocks of a given culture. If this wider process is not undertaken, the attempt to inculturate the priest will make him an odd sort of person representing a community which has not itself been radically inculturated and acculturated.

Priestly identity

Today, after Vatican II, no priest will be a spiritual person unless he has meditated in a profound and lengthy way on the meaning of the priestliness of Jesus. In other words, unless Jesus is at the centre of what a priest lives and does, the *tria munera* will have only cosmetic meaning. There are, indeed, many Christologies and there will be in the future many Christologies. The mystery of Jesus remains, even in our faith, a mystery. Nonetheless, the priest who longs to be a spiritual person must read and re-read the gospels. This should be the one book in a priest's possession that is dog-eared and wearing out. Again and again, a priest must ask anew: what is, from my own priestly view, the mission and ministry of Jesus? What do such words as 'kingdom' and 'the poor have the good news preached to them' mean for my priestly spirituality? What is the meaning of Church as the sacrament of Jesus? Are priests – am I as a priest – a sacrament of Jesus or am I a sacrament of hierarchy? Do I say glibly: 'I am a priest', or do I rather say: 'I believe I am a priest'?

Priestly spirituality in the future will not be related to some 'ontological' difference, a theological term which has had its day. Theologians, from the high scholastic period onward, have attempted to connect this ontological difference with sacramental character, but one would have to say that baptism creates an ontological difference and confirmation creates an ontological difference, which no theologian says. Still, our theology of baptism and confirmation tells us that in and through these sacraments we have been radically changed, more so indeed than a change which might occur at ordination.

In all of this, it is obvious that priestly spirituality can only be thought through and understood, and, for that matter, lived, when priestly spirituality and priestly life are not viewed in isolation, but within the very meaning of the gospels, of faith, of the Christian Church, of the Kingdom of God. In short, an isolated understanding of priestly spirituality is a deformed priestly spirituality. Within the parameters of this present essay, it is impossible to present such an integrated, non-isolationist approach. I have been able only to indicate key facts and issues which need this contextualization.

Priestly spirituality in the future will be much more embedded in the way in which Jesus lived his mission and ministry. When people hear in the Church and especially in the Church ministers, at every level, an echo of Jesus who proclaims the presence of the reign of God now, and who brings the unending compassion of God to the poor and the marginalized, only then will they truly say: our priestly servant leaders are holy. They are holy, not because of their own holiness, but because they are icons of the One Lord and the One Priest, Jesus.

NOTES

1. Cf. K. Osborne, *Priesthood* (New York: Paulist Press, 1988), pp. 307–42 for the background and explanation of this change in understanding of priesthood at Vatican II.
2. For a presentation and analysis of this Vatican II discussion, cf. the observations in the commentaries on *Presbyterorum Ordinis*, e.g. J. Lecuyer, 'Decree on the Ministry and Life of Priests: history of the Decree' in *Commentary on the Documents of Vatican II* (New York: Herder and Herder, 1969), vol. 4, pp. 183–209; B. Kloppenburg, *The Ecclesiology of Vatican II* (Chicago: Franciscan Herald Press, 1974), pp. 263–93; A. Ancel, *Il sacerdote secondo il Concilio Vaticano II* (Vicenza: Edizioni Favero, 1966); A. de Bovis, 'Le Presbytérat, sa nature et sa mission d'après le Concile Vatican II', *Nouvelle Revue Théologique* 89 (1967), pp. 1009–42; F. Marty, 'Decret sur le ministère et la vie de prêtres' in *Documents Conciliaires* (Paris: Centurion), vol. 4, pp. 159–82.
3. Cf. Osborne, op. cit., pp. 315–24, 333–7.
4. *Presbyterorum Ordinis*, no. 12.
5. Ibid., no. 12.
6. Ibid., no. 12.
7. Ibid., no. 13.
8. Ibid., no. 14.
9. Ibid., nos 15–17. As regards the intervention of Paul VI on the issue of priestly spirituality, cf. Osborne, op. cit., pp. 336–7.
10. On the relationship between the priesthood of all believers and ordained priesthood, which in the aftermath of Vatican II has been sharply discussed and debated, cf. K. Osborne, *Ministry* (New York: Paulist Press, 1993), pp. 535–7, 540–64.
11. NCCB, *As One Who-Serves* (Washington, DC: USCC, 1977).
12. Ibid., pp. 68–74.
13. Ibid., pp. 19–22.
14. Ibid., p. 19; the citation in the text is from W. Kasper, 'A new dogmatic outlook on the priestly ministry', *Concilium* 3.5 (1969), p. 14.
15. *As One Who Serves*, op. cit., p. 21.
16. Ibid., p. 21.
17. Ibid., p. 21.
18. Ibid., pp. 21–2.
19. *Formation of Priests in Circumstances of the Present Day*, authorized ET: NCCB (Washington, DC: USCC, 1990).
20. Cf. sections 10 to 13, which follow the outline from *Presbyterorum Ordinis*.
21. Ibid., 14.
22. Robert Schwartz, *Servant Leaders of the People of God* (New York: Paulist Press, 1989), p. 213.
23. Ibid., p. 215.
24. Schwartz concludes his observations, and indeed concludes the book itself, speaking only about the last dimension: namely, the distinctive priestly identity. He does this under the titles of (a) context, (b) activity and (c) goal. Under these three titles, the human identity and the baptized/eucharistic Christian identity are not treated at all, so that the integration of the specifically priestly identity with these two other, more fundamental, sources is passed over in silence.

Reconciliation

8

PATRICK PURNELL SJ

I feel a bitterness and hatred towards those that killed my father. At the same time I realise, as my father would have done, that there's a bigger question. The infection in this society has got hold of everyone. We all have blood on our hands. When it comes to thoughts of revenge I feel that I have to put it all behind me. (Gary McMichael, Lisburn, County Antrim)[1]

CHRISTIANE BRUSSELMANS WRITES 'How often parents say to a child words such as, "It's alright now. Just don't do that again." By forgiving their children, parents are teaching them what forgiving is and what forgiveness means. Parents are already instructing their children to the meaning of the sacrament of reconciliation.' And later in the same book, 'At the beginning of each eucharistic celebration, they join with all present in asking God to forgive them. When they give one another the sign of peace at mass, they are asking to be reconciled with others.'[2]

Christiane always situates her teaching of the sacraments in children's experience. What happens in their everyday lives is the door through which they walk into the mystery of the sacraments and the celebration of the sacraments illuminates the meaning of what happens in everyday life. What I want to explore in this chapter is how asking for and offering forgiveness belongs to the very heart of all human relationships and how, without forgiveness, we could not live together and deal with one another. We are always saying 'sorry' to one another with differing degrees of meaning and intensity. We continually hear 'I forgive you!' or 'Forget it! It doesn't matter!' We need this exchange for life to go on, in order for the

82

intricate mesh of human communications to survive. When we have said 'sorry' and do not hear we are forgiven, our lives are thwarted and frustrated; we are left searching for some way to reunite us to people. Reconciliation is at the heart of humanity's survival.

We live in a land of becoming. Our God is the Creator God. Creation proceeds stage by stage, step by step, in its long slow evolutionary process; creation is a becoming – a coming to be, a being born. We are called to be what God wants us to be. The 'call' is the call of a compassionate and generous God who binds each person to God's very self. It is the call of a God who longs for women and men to choose freely and lovingly to be one with God and to be one with one another in such a way that together we live as one family mirroring the unity of God, the Creator, the Word and the Spirit. Generation after generation have been invited to respond to the call to personify the mercy, compassion and justice of the Creator Lord and labour with God in the unfolding of creation. Divine Wisdom entrusted this great cosmic process of evolution to our care to be God's co-creators. We were appointed channels of life and love to one another. We were to love one another into the fullness of life and support and enable one another to reach the fullness of our humanity. But in sharing this life-giving power with us, the Creator took the prodigious and staggering risk of giving us the freedom to diminish and destroy God's awesome handi-work. As well as giving life, it became possible for us to deal death!

Humanity is, therefore, something we communicate to one another; it is a necessary transaction between people. We have the power to be to one another a source of life or a source of death. Thus we have power through acts of love or lovelessness literally to create or destroy one another. Through the creative power of love we can *bring-each-other-into-well-being*. Through the misuse of this power we can thwart life and maim each other. We can bring into being one community of truth, love, peace and justice, humanity's highest and greatest goal; or create hell's chaos. The fateful choice is ours, either to set free the power of God's love in the world so that together we form the nucleus of community or to deprive each other of the very basis of personhood and community. It is within the power of human love to build up dignity and self-respect in each other or to tear each other down and hurl each other into the abyss of being a nobody.

We are a race of sinners. We are a people who fail. Every age has its own sins or, perhaps, it would be more accurate to say, has its own particular expressions of sin because the basic ingredients of sin have remained constant from Adam to this day: pride, greed, covetousness, meanness of spirit, hatred, lust and so on. It is these evils which invade humanity's conscious and unconscious self.

Sin is both personal and social. It is personal in that each one of us can say 'I am a sinner!' It is social because we who sin are God's co-creators. When we sin we deliberately choose not to co-operate in God's work; we refuse to act as channels of life and love to one another and as a result of that choice, the damage we do and the harm we cause permeates the whole of humanity. Sin pervades nations and societies; it lodges in the systems and the structures which we create in order to organize ourselves as a society and as a nation.

It is because we sin, because we harm God's work, that God created forgiveness, the daughter of Wisdom:

> Although she [Wisdom] is alone, she can do everything; herself unchanging, she renews the world, and, generation after generation, passing into holy souls, she makes them into God's friends ... (Wisdom 7.27)

Wisdom renews the world; she makes people into God's friends. Forgiveness is God's gift to humanity. When Jesus was in a house in Capernaum, some people brought to him their friend who was a paralytic.

> Jesus saw their faith, and said to the paralytic, 'Take heart, son, your sins are forgiven.' Then some of the scribes said to themselves, 'This man is blaspheming.' And some thought, 'Who but God can forgive sin?' Knowing what was in their minds, Jesus said ... 'But so that you may know the Son of Man has authority on earth to forgive sins' – he then said to the paralytic – 'Stand up, take your bed and go to your home.' And he stood up and went to his home. When the crowds saw it, they were filled with awe, and they glorified God, who had given such authority to human beings. (cf. Matt 9:2–8 and Mark 2:7)

If God's awesome plan of creation was to be fulfilled and if humanity was to survive, humanity would have to learn to use the creative tool of forgiveness; the future would only be assured through forgiveness. There could be no way forward for creation unless women and men continually offered each other forgiveness; forgiveness belongs to the very essence of human relationships. Heaven and earth are joined; what is done on earth is done in heaven; God's power becomes ours.

At that solemn hour, 'In the evening of that same day, the first day of the week', Easter Day, the first day of the new creation, Jesus encapsulated the very heart of his mission and handed on his mission of reconciliation to those who had followed him, whom the Creator God, his Father, had given him,

> In the evening of that same day, the first day of the week, the doors were closed in the room where the disciples were for fear of the Jews. Jesus came and stood among them. He said to them, 'Peace be with you,' and after saying this, he showed them his hands and his side. The disciples were filled with joy at seeing the Lord, and he said to them again, 'Peace be with you. As the Father sent me, so am I sending you.' After saying this he breathed on them and said: 'Receive the Holy Spirit. If you forgive anyone's sins, they are forgiven; if you retain anyone's sins, they are retained.' (John 20:19–23)

What God was establishing through Jesus (the Creator's Son who knew the mind of the Creator) at that moment was a people who would be reconcilers, to whom God gave the divine power to forgive; a people who would recognize that forgiveness is located at the heart of all human relationships and at the centre of their mission to renew the face of the earth. Not to forgive is the way of destruction and death; unforgiven sin becomes one's own sin; by not forgiving we take ownership of the offence; *they* (sins) *are retained.*

This was the mission Jesus committed to his followers: they were to teach people to forgive. They were to use the gift of forgiveness they had received from their Creator to re-create and transform the world.

The classical portrayal of reconciliation is Jesus' story of the Prodigal Son (Luke 15) which they, his friends and followers, heard from his lips. The son returns; hunger and misery drive him home; 'At least he'll have me back as one of the hired hands', he thought; but there at home the unbearable love of a grieving father was awaiting him. The son could bear being a hired hand; there would be something just about being a serving man, a way of paying a debt which would save some shreds of self-respect and dignity; but to be 'son' ... That was something he could not be without a transformation he could not work in himself. And so the father, the victim, humiliated by his son's ingratitude, clothed him: 'Quick! Bring out the best robe and put it on him; put a ring on his finger and sandals on his feet' (Luke 15:22).

Reconciliation is rooted in the terrible love of God that is irresistible – a love that can break down and overcome all barriers. Paul proclaims with astonishment 'he died for us while we were still sinners' (Rom 5:8). God loved us when we were enemies. Such indeed is God's love! But while we may desire to be the recipients of such a love, we question in our inner selves the terrible paradox of a God, the victim of sin, being its absolution.

What, then, of the victim of sin, the victim of oppression and exploitation? Of abuse, brutality and violence? Of unkindness, lies and humiliation? Of sexual harassment and defamation of character? Sin of its nature causes harm and unhappiness and the gravity of sin can be measured by the amount of harm and unhappiness it inflicts upon the victim. What, then, in the whole process of reconciliation is the place of the victims? Are the victims to be fully compensated, as if you could compensate the victims of apartheid or the victim whose limbs have been mangled by torture, or even the victims of defamation, jealousy, and lust? Does reconciliation offer a divine way by which everything is restored to what it was before the offence was committed?

And the answer to this question is 'No!' Because the victim is co-creator! God's act of reconciling the world to God's self is the raising of Jesus Christ from the dead but the Christ who is raised is not a miraculously reconstituted Jesus Christ. The Risen One is victim! The evangelists insist: 'He showed them his hands and his feet' (Luke 24:39). 'Put your finger here; look, here are my hands. Give me your hand, put it in my side' (John 20:27). The risen Jesus is the wounded Jesus. Everything cannot be as it once was, as if everything could be blotted out and we could continue as if nothing had ever happened. The Christ who is today present in our lives, the Christ whom we celebrate in our Eucharist is Victim, the wounded Christ. The story we receive is the story of one who will forever bear the wounds of human ingratitude and those who are 'in Christ' will share in his woundedness. The co-creator is the co-victim.

The past cannot be obliterated; the 'new' has to emerge out of the 'old'. Far back in Israel's story the prophet Isaiah discerned that woundedness has the power to heal, 'We have been healed by his bruises' (Isaiah 53:5). A new humanity evolves out of the broken pieces of the old; there is no other possible way forward. The only hope for the world lies in the possibility that death, destruction, devastation, pride, jealousy, anger, lust can become the bearers of new life. That is why forgiveness is central to the dynamic of creation. The victim is called upon to create through the act of forgiveness a future not only for her/himself but also for and with the sinner and for the world which has been violated by sin. The victim through her/his wounds is the one who offers pardon; the wounded one becomes the healer.

'When they had eaten, Jesus said to Simon Peter, "Simon son of John, do you love me more than these others do?" ' (John 21:15). He put this question about love to Simon three times, naming him, 'Simon son of John', the name by which he had been known before he had called him into his company and dubbed him 'Rock'. Three denials! Three protestations of love! What he had done, the crime he had committed, could never be undone; it was part of his story and had to be remembered. Yet through forgiveness and love, it became the paradoxical cement of his renewed friendship with the Christ. It would degrade forgiveness if sin were wiped out, obliterated and forgotten as if it had never existed. The immensity and greatness of God's love is such, that God loves us as sinners, as criminals. Sin is an intrinsic element of our journey; we are what we are as much as the result of our sins as of our good deeds. Our story is the story of a sinner from birth to this moment of our lives. We are loved sinners. The only way forward is the way of the forgiven sinner who employs the creative tool of forgiveness.

As the world watches the transition in South Africa from apartheid to a multi-racial democracy, we hear the words of Nelson Mandela: 'Men of peace must not think about retribution or recriminations. Courageous people do not fear forgiveness for the sake of peace.' A new community is beginning to emerge in which black and white alike are struggling to enter a culture in which apartheid is defined as a crime against humanity. They enter this society as oppressive agents and victims of apartheid; oppressors and victims alike are going to have to learn to live together as one people, one community, owning and neither forgetting nor denying a past stained by horrific abuses of human rights. In this community the past has to be named, the truth revealed. The victim must be given a hearing. Herein lies the key to, the cornerstone of the healing process – the wound must be exposed before it can be cured; hiding the truth prevents national reconciliation by denying the victims the chance to forgive. And even though the culprits will be forgiven and not punished, what they did will not be forgotten. Only thus can a culture of discrimination, oppression and violence give way to a culture in which God's reign can take root.

The Church is the servant of God's reign and makes known to the world the saving activity of Jesus. In the liturgical reforms of the Second Vatican Council, the Church developed ways of celebrating the sacrament of reconciliation. The insights which these reforms are struggling to express are precisely those which are being so richly embodied in the transition taking place in South Africa. Christiane Brusselmans reflects 'When they give one another the sign of peace at mass, they are asking to be reconciled with others'.[3] The Church offers us a community in which to come to terms with the past and it enables us to create a new future. Somehow or other we need to express this in sacramental form. We need to recognize our relationship to society and our responsibility for one another. Sin is not something we do in some private corner; we who sin are God's co-creators; sin infiltrates and harms the whole of society. We need to be able to articulate (and be seen to articulate) our sinfulness and to receive (and be seen to receive) the pardon of the community in the absolution from the community pronounced by the priest representing the community, so that in the very act of loving and being reconciled to one another we are reconciled to God. And in this sacrament know and understand that where sin abounded, grace abounds still more, and in being graced by the faith community we are healed.

NOTES

Biblical quotations are taken from the Jerusalem Bible (London: Darton, Longman and Todd, 1966).

1. From the *Observer Magazine* (13 March 1994).
2. Christiane Brusselmans and Brian A. Haggerty, *We Celebrate Reconciliation* (Atlanta: Silver Burdett, 1976).
3. Ibid.

Time in the sacraments and the liturgical year

9

SUSAN K. ROLL

IRONICALLY, in the United States more than in any other country up to now, the Order for the Christian Initiation of Adults has amply proven its worth not simply as a more integrated, personal and participative approach to Christian initiation than the earlier, highly cognitive 'convert class', but as a vehicle for renewal and dynamic revitalization within an entire parish community. One might ordinarily think that the Order would catch on more in countries in which large numbers of persons have not had access to the Christian faith, or for whom obstacles had been placed in the way: mission territories in Africa and Asia for example, or in the new republics of the former Soviet Union, where numbers of adults are baptized, often with only minimal preparation.

Perhaps one of the reasons for the success of the OCIA (and here we are using the term OCIA, formerly RCIA, to cover the entire process in its four stages of hospitality/inquiry, instruction, illumination and mystagogy, and not just the liturgical rites of the *Ordo* itself) is the relative openness among Americans to self-awareness. Self-help groups addressing all sorts of addictions, disorders, traumas and personality difficulties thrive, and some of the better-established groups such as Alcoholics Anonymous find a haven in the facilities of parish churches. In a time when the traditional sacrament of reconciliation is rarely sought out in its ritual form, sincerely motivated persons are struggling to heal their private wounds and to forgive those who were involved in the pain in their past, as well as learning to forgive themselves and to undertake continual conversion to a healthier, wiser way of life.

One central element which underlies both the OCIA and the need for healing and forgiveness, and also (as we will be addressing in this article) the feasts of the liturgical year, is the metaphor of the journey. A journey, by its nature, moves in an irreversible progression: 'You can't go home again', or if you do, it will somehow be different, and more to the point, *you* will be different. This fact underscores not only the personal, variable and dynamic nature of the faith journey (Christiane Brusselmans used to insist to her students that the OCIA is a *process*, not a *programme*; we were constantly on guard lest the 'P-word' should accidentally drop from our lips), but also the necessity on the macro-scale of the Church for structures flexible and adaptable enough to permit healthy growth processes on the part of local churches, parish communities, small faith-sharing groups and individual Christians. From this perspective we can take a newer approach to the liturgical year more consistent with the global shift in thinking regarding sacramental preparation, of which the OCIA is the paradigm. But in order to do that, we first have to examine the main current of twentieth-century thought on the experience of time in liturgy with relation to the theology of the liturgical year – and turn it on its head.

THE PASCHAL MYSTERY AS FOCAL POINT

A superficial examination of the origins of the Christian calendar of feasts might suggest that the concept of the liturgical year as an entity in itself was in place far earlier than it really was. The first few generations of Christians celebrated only the weekly anniversary of Christ's resurrection, the first day of the week (also called the 'eighth day' of the week in a deliberately outside-of-time, eschatological perspective). By the middle of the second century the Easter feast, whose date was calculated not according to the solar Julian calendar but still following the basically lunar Jewish calendar, was well enough established to occasion sharp controversy concerning whether the feast should be celebrated precisely on 14 Nisan to coincide with the Jewish Passover, or on the following Sunday. A group of Asian Christians who followed a version of the Julian calendar set the date arbitrarily on 6 April. At that point the Christian Pascha celebrated not simply the resurrection but a wide sweep of the mystery of redemption, beginning with the incarnation (Talley, 1990, pp. 5–11). Lent as a period for prebaptismal catechesis and formation is attested by the *Apostolic*

Tradition in the first half of the third century, and as the traditional 'forty days' fast shortly after the Council of Nicaea (Talley, 1990, pp. 163–8). The feast of Christmas is first attested on a Roman calendar only in 336 CE, and from about 380 was instituted in the East, where an Epiphany feast with multiple themes was already customary. The commemoration of the feast days of martyrs and saints can be traced back to the middle of the second century when Christians arranged to gather for a picnic meal at the tomb of a martyr on the anniversary of the person's date of death (or 'birthday into heaven'), following the Roman custom of commemorating deceased family members.

Yet lining up the origins for specific feasts does not point to any early unified concept of 'the liturgical year'. The first reference to the 'church year' (*Kirchenjahr*) comes from a Lutheran preacher, Johannes Pomarius (Baumgart), in 1589. The term 'Christian year' appears in France in the seventeenth century, and by the nineteenth century Dom Prosper Guéranger entitled his massive work *The Liturgical Year* (*Année liturgique*). Other terms used by various scholars which tended to suggest a pre-given integrated liturgical year include 'year of salvation' and 'year of the Lord', while designations such as 'the sanctification of time' or simply 'the Christian feasts' loosen the individual feasts from their overall framework. All of these however date from the twentieth century.

Thus the notion of a theologically integrated liturgical year centred on the paschal mystery is of relatively recent vintage. The earliest schemas and divisions of the cycle of yearly feasts, dating from the thirteenth and fourteenth centuries, are partial and leave gaps in sequence. The post-Tridentine Roman Missal of 1570 begins the Church year with the first Sunday of Advent and concludes with the 24th Sunday after Pentecost, illustrating that the Church now had in place a notion of a 'year' separate from the civil calendar, but still operating on a linear concept. Up to the early twentieth century the liturgical year was primarily perceived as a didactic tool to promote the moral instruction of the faithful by exhorting them to pattern themselves after the example of Jesus in his earthly life (Auf der Maur, 1983, pp. 211–12).

Dom Odo Casel (d. 1948), a monk of the Benedictine foundation at Maria-Laach, introduced radical new thinking concerning the mystery-centred nature of the presence of Christ in liturgical celebrations inspired by parallels with what was known of ancient Greek mystery religions. For Casel the Paschal mystery represented the centre from which the entire liturgical year radiated: the Easter event was thus not merely a historical anniversary celebration which played off collective memory and community identity, but an actualization of the living Christ present in an inexplicable but pervasive and profound manner.

Casel's thought represented a leap forward in the development of the concept of the liturgical year, consonant with the findings of liturgical historians concerning the earliest Paschal centrality of Christian celebration. The idea (or at least the terminology) was adopted and set in the mainstream within a neo-scholastic framework in the 1947 papal encyclical *Mediator Dei* (although Casel's school of thought remained highly suspect in Rome). In *Mediator Dei* the *cyclus mysteriorum* of the Church year is intended to help the faithful participate in the living presence of Christ as Head of the Mystical Body, to receive the grace offered in the present by his salvific actions in the past, and to offer them a moral example to follow (this picks up the thread of the eighteenth- and nineteenth-century parenetic approach). Here the centrality of the Paschal mystery follows not yet from celebration, but from function: reflecting the paradigm of Christ as head of the Church in a pyramidical power schema, it serves to instruct the people and to mould their behaviour and attitudes. There is no consistent theology of the liturgical year worked out in the encyclical: it shifts from a Christocentric notion to a moralizing function, to a salvation history/presence model (not derived from 'new authors', but extracted from scholastic principles) (Auf der Maur, 1983, pp. 223-6).

The Constitution on the Sacred Liturgy of the Second Vatican Council, *Sacrosanctum Concilium* (SC), laid down much clearer and more consistent principles for a centralized, closed-system theology of the liturgical year. SC employs the concepts of memorial celebration and anamnesis to retain the notion of the abiding presence of Christ – 'Thus recalling the mysteries of the redemption, [the Church] opens up to the faithful the riches of her Lord's powers and merits, so that these are in some way made present for all time' (SC 102) – while minimizing the imposed pedagogical–moral and thus functional value of celebrating the yearly feasts. Here the centrality of the Paschal mystery becomes a principle of thorough reform: the Sunday celebration, 'the foundation and kernel of the whole liturgical year' (SC 106), takes priority over the accumulation of saints' days and minor feasts. Similarly Easter, as the celebration *par excellence* of Christ's salvific death and resurrection, is affirmed in its eschatological as well as its memorial dimensions. The distinctive characteristics of each liturgical season are to be 'preserved or restored to suit the conditions of modern times', but in any case the Paschal season with its preparation in Lent retains pride of place.

Indeed since Vatican II, and fully in line with SC's injunction to restore the baptismal features which had fallen into disuse in connection with Lent so that the season would serve as both a reminder of and a preparation for baptism among the worshipping community, the restored rites of the OCIA realize and put into motion a renewed catechumenal practice, and happily at the same time a revitalization of the baptized people of God. The deeper roots of this Paschal restoration lie further back than the practices of the early Church: they connect with the importance of the Exodus as the constitutive founding event of the Hebrew people, as celebrated in the Pesach, the Passover feast. Symbolic extensions into Christianity include Christ as the 'Passover lamb' who was sacrificed for us, whose blood sets us free. Thus the vision of SC formed both a link with, and a necessary contextualization of, Casel's thought on Paschal centrality, letting go of both the ancient Greek mystery-model in Casel and the scholastic categories in *Mediator Dei* while opening wide to a celebration model of the liturgical year. Future directions, if the same line of thought is maintained, could include a deepening of the liberation theme with contemporary concrete application to the pain and hope of oppressed peoples, and a strengthening of awareness that humanity is of a piece with all creation (Auf der Maur, 1983, pp. 226-8).

The issue that we need to address specifically however is that of centrality – the fixing of a centre point from which all else radiates – as an organizing principle for the liturgical year, and its implications. The gradual shift toward perceiving the Paschal mystery, the core of the original Gospel message, as the nucleus not only from which the structure of the liturgical year radiates but in which all the sacraments, and most profoundly baptism, find their meaning, seems at first glance to point to a more sophisticated, better integrated, higher level of evolution than the notion of a series of unconnected separate feast days, or separate sacraments with variably articulated scriptural roots. Yet shifts in perception rarely occur in a vacuum; they evolve from and contribute toward currents of thought in the wider social context, secular as well as ecclesial.

What would lead to a global shift toward a central organizing principle, why would it make sense, or a bit more pointedly, what interests would be served? A clue can be found back in *Mediator Dei*, in its link between the Paschal mystery as the summit of the Church year, and the 'Headship of

Christ' over the Body, the baptized members of the Church. The 'head-ship' paradigm translates quickly into applications to the exercise of power and structural superiority of some members of the Body over others, when hierarchy and rank according to status or power function as a key metaphor. Already in the fourth century as the Christian Church came out from 'underground' following the Edict of Milan, and in its newly safe environment began to take on some of the mentality of the secular Roman Empire against which Christians had previously defined their own iden-tity, one sees domination and power-metaphors more and more applied to Christ. Worship of the sun as the supreme cosmic power had been officially established in Rome in 275 by the emperor Aurelian, who was himself declared a god after the model of Oriental divine emperors. In the fourth and early fifth centuries references to Christ as the 'Sun of Justice' (from Malachi 3:20) and other sun comparisons reflect a notion that Christ is perceived through the same analogical lens as ruler, lord, king and dominator of all (*pantocrator*), from whom intense power radiates like the rays of the sun. By the mid-fifth century, in the wake of a political power vacuum left in the Empire by weak and ineffectual emperors, Pope Leo the Great was able to negotiate successfully with invading Germanic peoples to spare Rome, with the functional authority of the head of state; the same Leo made appeal to Matthew 16:18 to justify the headship of the Bishop of Rome over the patriarchs of other major sees such as Jerusalem, Con-stantinople, Alexandria and Antioch. In other words, the social–cultural setting which promoted the paradigm of a single glorious divine male ruler exercising supreme power seeped into the Church and affected both how the risen Christ was perceived, and the governmental structures of the Church and their underlying rationale.

Because of the twentieth century's horrendous experiences of fascism, totalitarianism, total war, genocide and ongoing ecocide, one needs to ask whether the paradigm of a central organizing principle to which total power and domination is ascribed inherently carries within it the seeds of destruction and death. Placing the problem on this scale may seem way out of proportion in a genteel consideration of the feasts of the Christian year, but in fact what we celebrate are paradigms, primordial patterns, norma-tive traditions and stories about 'how the world is', and, more importantly, 'how the world can become'. The given meaning of traditional religious celebrations becomes woven into our psyches from an early age, and persists long after we no longer think to articulate them again, but simply plan the liturgies and prepare the feast.

THE LITURGICAL YEAR AS A SEQUENCE

More fundamental to the way in which Christians experience and celebrate the liturgical year, however, is our experience of the rhythms of
time. The most classic (and classically overused) scheme is that derived by
the anthropologist of religion Mircea Eliade from research into a variety of
pre-literate cultures, together with a generalization of their characteristic
religious forms, myths and festivals. The traditional festivals make the
founding myth of the culture present again, enable present-day worshippers to be inserted into the mysteries, and on a cosmic scale allow a sort
of return to the origins, the sacred pristine time in which everything was
freshly created: an example is the wild chaos of New Year's parties and
revelry, followed by sober New Year's resolutions intended, in some way,
to create the world anew. In this sense sacred time is 'reversible': human
religious acts not only call to memory but re-actualize the divine roots of
the particular human culture and its distinctive identity as a community
within the natural world and within the nexus of divine beings.

Eliade isolated two differing global perceptions of time with bearing
upon the celebration of religious feasts: *cyclical* and *linear* time. The cycle of
yearly feasts corresponds on a deep unconscious or subconscious level to
the human person's life rhythms within a matrix of cosmic life-rhythms:
the cycles of the sun and the moon mark time, as do the agricultural and
climatic seasons, cycles of fertility in animals and humans, even the simple
rhythm of heartbeat, of breathing oxygen in and carbon dioxide out in
opposite rhythm to that of green plants and trees. Cyclical time folds back
on itself, it renews and purifies itself, just as the periodic celebration of
traditional religious festivals mark an anchoring-point in the cycle, a point
to which to return, a point not chosen capriciously by human beings but
determined by the cosmic powers and rooted in absolute reality (Eliade,
1959, pp. 68–91).

The tendency, especially among Christian liturgists, has been to over-
simplify this schema, to identify *cyclical* perception of religious time with
'primitive', 'pagan', and therefore less worthy cultures, and *linear* time with
a proposed definitive shift in time-perception among the ancient Hebrew
and later Christian peoples. Here linear time is associated with the events
of salvation history: the Jewish Passover and the Christian Easter do not re-
create these events on a cosmic eternal scale, but they serve as an
'anamnesis', a defence against forgetting the founding-events in history of
the people of God. The *Haggadah*, the book of the Passover Seder, repeats

'And you shall tell your child on that day', and Christians recall in the Eucharistic Prayer the words of Jesus, 'Whenever you do this, do it in memory of me'. For many anthropologists of religion cyclical time is conceived as an eternal closed loop, a dead-end in perpetual motion, compared with the sense of meaningful movement embodied in Judaeo-Christian linear time: the rich meaning of historical events in the past points to an eschatological future, hoped-for yet unknown.

This leaves one fundamental paradox with which liturgists must contend: the fact that Christians continue the rhythmic cyclical celebration of feasts linked in an anniversaristic way with events in salvation history. The feasts recur weekly or annually, the events themselves happened once uniquely in the past. The similarly overused solution is to employ a conjunction of both schemas: a spiral, which loops round on itself yet moves forward with each cycle, never exactly repeating the past, yet not as direct and unambiguous as a straight line. For most this represents a satisfactory solution and is taught as the definitive model for the contemporary perception of religious time. Yet just as with the Paschal centrality of the feasts of the liturgical year, we need to go deeper and to ask more penetrating questions based on the lived experience of a journey of continual conversion in community in the OCIA, continually doing a 'reality check' with insights coming out of contemporary critical theology, most notably feminist and liberation-minded currents.

Even from the vantage point of its integrative conclusion in 'the spiral', the act of setting up a conceptual schema of linear versus cyclical time involves the construction of a dualism, an either/or, black/white, on/off, yes/no binary model which in itself allows of no nuancing, shading, natural growth process, internal dynamism or dynamism in dialogue with the surrounding environment. Dualisms are neat, clean, predictable, controllable sorting mechanisms for random phenomena. They also, inconveniently, tend to force phenomena into categories which serve the needs of the cohesion of the overall schema but do not adequately reflect the multifaceted complex nature of the given reality itself. More dangerously, dualisms masquerade as objective cognitive tools for simplifying complex realities down to their basic framework: in a dualistic binary schema one supposedly equal factor is set over against another, and each is more distinctly defined by means of the contrast.

The truth is, however, that dualisms by their nature tend to devolve into a value-ranking of one pole as superior to the other, depending upon which persons, or groups of persons, have the power to define the polarity and set up the terms. The very act of exerting intellectual mastery by imposing binary contrast-definitions works automatically in favour of those who possess the prerogative of doing so. The poetic image of light versus darkness which pervades much of Christian Scripture, mysticism, poetry, and liturgical symbolism takes on a very different cast when one applies it to skin colour: is light skin better/more worthy/more enlightened than dark skin? Who defines the terms and their relative value? What does a dark-skinned person feel when 'light' in the abstract is automatically valued over 'dark'? In the same way, if a religious person in the Judaeo-Christian salvation-history tradition defines 'primitive' cyclical versus more 'enlightened' linear time perception, bringing them together in a spiral figure does not erase the fundamental valuational bias – at best it might obscure it. The basic dualistic split and the drive for intellectual mastery and control which acts to justify it remain unchallenged, and the subjective vantage point of the person or persons doing the defining is not perceived as exerting a bias.

A JOURNEY IN TIME

Let us take the 'journey of conversion' metaphor of the OCIA as a starting point, and see whether we can end up at a more credible, honest, comprehensive conclusion. Undeniably there is a strong linear aspect to a journey, whether a form of travel from town A to town B, or a life's journey. As we said right at the start, one cannot go home again – the unfolding dynamism of time, place, and the configuration of living beings, other persons, is such that no *Gestalt* repeats itself. There is a time-bound irreversibility involved in a journey. One can go back to the same geographic place, but not to the original time. (By way of contrast, two people can occupy the same time together, but not, physically, the same space.) One can reverse the spatial direction of the journey, but the total lived situation is different – the least one can say is that some time has passed and the living beings involved are somewhat older.

This means that the belief in the eternal reversibility of sacred time which Eliade's schema ascribes to pre-literate cultures is simply an impossibility – and that will tend to make such cultures appear more 'primitive' and naïve than ever. But it also means that a naïve belief in the infinite projection and prolongation of linear time is also an impossibility, or more specifically that effective human control and predictability over the time of the future is impossible. Both history and eschatology escape human control; one cannot fully know the past, considering how much data is lost and how much selective forgetting can occur, individually and collectively, nor the future. Similarly one can change neither the past nor, considering that it comes as a package in a yet-to-be-specified context, the future. Over the centuries various small gnostic groups have believed that they could ascertain precisely the time when the world would end, and they would gather on hilltops and wait ... and wait ... There are fundamentalists who still believe that, any day now, the Rapture will suddenly sweep them up from their daily tasks into eternal glory – them, and no one else.

One among the many gifts of the OCIA to the local church communities which undertake to invite, teach and escort their catechumens together, is the gift of learning to let go of preplanned agendas for the Holy Spirit and programmed curricula designed to control and channel the accumulation of cognitive knowledge in the hope that the heart and spirit will manage to trundle along behind the mind. This is what is meant by 'process, not programme'. Inquirers and catechumens progress as they feel called, ready and strengthened to do so, within a supportive context of Christian community. The persons' whole life-histories up to the present, the way in which their history unfolds in all aspects of their lives, their families and intimate relations, even the way in which they are affected by political, social, cultural, or professional/labour-related factors, all enter into the complex deepening of faith and the awareness of God's living presence in the depth of one's being. The premiss of the OCIA, both the overall process and the progression of the rites themselves, embodies an openness to gratuitous time, time lived in dialogue with the will of a loving, trustworthy God. Genuine growth and progress is not always linear and sequential – sometimes it resembles more the procession of Echternach, 'two steps forward, one step back', or let us say even a few steps sideways. Sometimes it seems to explode in all directions; insights and discoveries from one aspect of one's life reverberate and transform other aspects and relations. The linear paradigm may have more to do with assumptions rooted in the Enlightenment about continual human progress and improvement, always in some way under human conscious control. By contrast, authentic growth in dialogue with a loving divine wisdom, however one perceives that wisdom working in one's life and relations, can sometimes be frustratingly messy.

The feasts of the liturgical year cohere in a very rough sequence with the pivotal events in the life of Jesus – not always with historical accuracy, as witness the birthday feast of Jesus on 25 December for which there is no scriptural support, but nonetheless in a certain natural progression: he was expected, he was born, grew up, passed through formative experiences, faced both popular success and increasing difficulties, finally confronted condemnation and death, yet his life perdured in the life of the new *ecclesia* gathered in his name. Jesus lived on earth as we do, within an irreversible matrix of time, and his life events unfolded with much the same complexity as ours; if not, his life would have been less than fully human, and his death and resurrection less than fully redemptive. Here we come up against one of those necessary 'reality checks': Jesus did not begin his life with the resurrection and only later get born. Neither do we begin the liturgical year with the Easter Vigil, and let everything else devolve in a sequentially secondary sequence. In our own lives, we do not begin on our wedding day, nor the day of our greatest professional success; we begin at the God-given beginning and work our way through, one day to the next, not knowing whether the following day will be given to us as a gift from God or not. Each breath, each minute, each day is a gracious gift, never to return, and never to be taken for granted.

THE SACRAMENTAL JOURNEY AS GROWTH

Our own sacramental journey in the time of our own life takes place in the awareness of Jesus' fundamental solidarity with us. What the OCIA makes clear is that 'Jesus travels with us every step of the way from death to life' (Dunning, 1981, p. 31). Death to life? Isn't a reverse-linear process even more problematic than a straightforward one? Perhaps we need to better nuance our working paradigms: a journey does have a certain directionality about it, even one like the forty-year wandering of Moses and the Hebrew people in the desert – they did eventually wind up at a definitive endpoint. The model of growth envisioned and built into the structure of the OCIA involves moving through certain stages of initiation, albeit unique in their particular expression to each person, in a total configuration related to each local parish community. The lectionary readings for the liturgical year which form the basis for the catechumenal journey follow the life of Christ on earth during the festal seasons, then fill in the rest of the Sundays with stories and precepts from his teaching and healing work. Yet there remains a non-linear, transhistorical dimension to the journey, any journey. Because we are highly complex persons, living on different levels at any one time and full of unconscious and subconscious thoughts, images and motives, and on top of that constantly interacting with our at-least-equally complex human and natural environment, any schematic model for the life-journey necessarily suffers from oversimplification.

This could point up the usefulness of employing the contemporary language of God as 'Wisdom' as an interpretative key within the global faith-journey marked by the concrete symbolism and immediate tangibility of the sacraments. The Book of Wisdom in the deuterocanonical Hebrew Bible sets forth exquisite expressions of the beauty of wisdom:

> Wisdom is brilliant, she never fades. ... Meditating on her is understanding in its perfect form, and anyone keeping awake for her will soon be free from care. For she herself searches everywhere for those who are worthy of her, benevolently appearing to them on their ways, anticipating their every thought. For Wisdom begins with the sincere desire for instruction, anxiety for instruction means loving her, loving her means keeping her laws, attention to her laws guarantees incorruptibility, and incorruptibility brings us near to God. (Wisdom 6:12, 15–19)

Already fairly early in the life of the Church, the idea of Christ as Wisdom gradually evolved into a Logos Christology, leaving the Church effectively without the older, conceptually feminine image. Ultimately this resulted in a predominantly cognitive, transcendent notion of God which left little room to acknowledge the immanent God, the God who speaks wisdom clearly in our hearts if we listen, and who speaks wisdom to us through others. This wisdom element has in the past decade been consciously sought out and retrieved, particularly by feminist and eco-theological scholarship, and new forms of liturgy and prayer have been developed to celebrate the wisdom-facet of God.

For its part, the progressive instruction characteristic of the OCIA is based upon the unfolding of stories and their wisdom throughout the year in the Lectionary, as opposed to a more dogmatic, programmed, logo-centric 'convert class' approach. The rites which precede the sacraments of initiation – acceptance into the order of catechumens, election, the scrutinies – themselves embody a gradual opening to mystery, and touch the participants at a level deeper than words alone. In the OCIA the reception of the sacraments is ideally allowed to return to its historically natural sequence – baptism, confirmation, Eucharist as the crown, then somewhat later and according to readiness, reconciliation. Confirmation is linked more clearly and immediately with baptism, instead of constituting in effect a sacrament of 'graduation' from religion at an age when distancing oneself from the Church may simply be a temporary way to assert one's soon-to-be-adult independence (see Duggan and Kelly, 1991). This shift in structure and sequence of the sacraments testifies to a willingness to affirm the potential of each Christian or Christian-to-be to discern the path to which they are called, and the pace at which they move, in the wisdom of their own hearts and in the 'pooled wisdom', as it were, of a supportive community.

In this sense, the wisdom underlying our faith and embodied in Christ could be expressed, perhaps a bit simplistically, as 'let go and let God': that is to say, within a loving and supportive faith community in which each person is cherished as a gift of God, each one can walk the faith-journey, discern callings and yearnings, sort out options, make decisions, and share experiences and perceptions with others. This is why the length of time that one spends as a catechumen is elastic, depending on the discernment of the individual in the context of the community and together with a sponsor, not fixed in a rigid schedule (although the rites preliminary to initiation fit into the aforementioned Lenten framework).

This is also why an OCIA-type process can be adapted to welcome, support and reintegrate former Catholics who have left the Church for a variety of reasons, often many years before and often in frustration and deep anger. Proposals for such a parish-based 're-membering' process have deep historical roots in the ancient Order of Penitents, those who re-entered the community on Holy Thursday after expiating major public sins they had committed which had caused scandal in the community (see Favazza, 1989). The insights underlying the journey of initiation parallel those of a journey of healing, wholeness and welcome. In both cases the persons on the journey are supported by an entire substructure channelling the wisdom of God, internally and externally, expressed in all the complex dimensions in which we live and grow.

FLEXIBLE PRIORITIES

By way of conclusion, we can perhaps take the wisdom foundation underlying the dynamism and depth of the OCIA process and trace it in contemporary developments in thinking concerning the liturgical year.

We have looked at the questionable presuppositions behind the dominant model which would impose Paschal centrality as the only way to understand and live the feasts of the liturgical year. This is not by any means to diminish the fundamental kerygma of the Christian faith, nor to deny the importance of the hope of life in death, the primordial symbolism of dying and rising with Christ inherent in baptism, or its living memorial in the Eucharist.

Wisdom, however, may be broader, more varied, more dynamic and less controllable than we tend to think, and at a certain point wise theologians, catechists and liturgists need to ask, not what *must* the people of God think, believe or do, but what in fact *do* they think, believe or do. More than one pastor has noted that very many grassroots Catholics tend to work out their faith more from the perspective of incarnation, and less from redemption. Many would have difficulty explaining what it means to say that Christ died for our sins, or how his resurrection redeems us. And certainly in North America and parts of Europe, far more Christians, marginal Christians and persons with no discernible faith-commitment at all crowd the churches at midnight on Christmas Eve, out of a deep sense that this is a time that they want and need to be close to the presence of Christ, however dimly understood or sentimentally expressed. By contrast, in spite of the contribution made to the capital importance of the Easter Vigil by parishes which have instituted and inspired a vital OCIA process, in the popular mind Easter still often remains the 'second' feast of the liturgical year, a very fine spring holiday (spring in the northern hemisphere at any rate) which somehow misses the profound mystic, personal, familial meaning-freight of Christmas.

Posing the 'reality question' in this way should not imply an either/or dilemma concerning the comparative significance of Christmas and Easter: that would be a perfect example of a dualistic model set up in terms constructed by First World liturgists according to their own point of departure. By contrast, in countries where popular devotion has come under Spanish influence such as Mexico and the Philippines, Good Friday attracts massive popular participation, to the point that Easter Sunday is simply an anti-climax. These cultures tend to face death with fewer inbuilt qualms than Anglo-Saxon-linked cultures, and work through their fears and ambivalences as exemplified by the Mexican feast of the dead in November. In other regions various local saints' days or Marian feasts generate extraordinary enthusiasm and nourish commitment, on some level, to the faith. In some Western countries Ash Wednesday, which is not a holy day of obligation, inspires a sort of felt obligation on the part of numbers of even marginal Christians to go to church and 'get ashes'.

In order to bring the ideal and the real a bit closer together, one needs to apply the wise approach which characterizes both the pre-catechumenate and the earliest stage of a re-membering process: listening to each other's stories. Listening, letting others share the events of their journey to date, and truly listening in order to open oneself to the wisdom they have to share, entails an attitude of receptivity, a letting-go of unjustified power and control over others, a refusal to pass judgement or to impose rigid group-think on complex living human persons. The same, on a macro scale, holds true for a genuine inculturation of the feasts of the liturgical year in terms of the lived realities of often vastly different world cultures: listening to each other without overpowering the ones speaking, learning from each other in humility and caring, letting Christian praxis take shape and evolve with both fidelity to its deep historical roots and openness to flexibility in meeting the needs of the future, in each local context.

Moreover one needs to understand 'cultures' here not simply as counties with fixed boundaries, nor as tribal cultures within larger nations. Perhaps the most significant cultures which must be heard are those of women: numerically half of the human population, and considerably more than half of most Christian worshipping communities, women as women have been structurally excluded from all but peripheral participation in liturgy, and so rarely invited to reflect on aspects of liturgy in terms of the wisdom of their own lives that they find it hard at first even to know clearly what to think. Yet at present women's liturgies, often stunningly creative and brilliantly symbolic, are blossoming in many countries, and hold forth the potential to revitalize Christian liturgical practice and to make it far more articulate and authentic than ever in its history.

Ultimately both fully initiated Christians and Christians-to-be are thrown back on the need for a leap of faith – to believe that God is indeed real, that a greater intelligence than ours is at work in our lives and in the world around us, and that a greater wisdom with its own call and its own will speaks to us. The shape of the journey on which we are embarked, a journey of continual conversion which does not terminate with the reception of a formal sacrament but deepens and broadens in proportion to our openness to enter into it, cannot but lead us nearer to the living wisdom of the living God.

REFERENCES

Hansjörg Auf der Maur, *Feiern im Rhythmus der Zeit* I: *Herrenfeste in Woche und Jahr* (Gottesdienst der Kirche, Handbuch der Liturgiewissenschaft, vol. 5; Regensburg: Friedrich Pustet, 1983).

Christiane Brusselmans (ed.), *Toward Moral and Religious Maturity* (Morristown, NJ: Silver Burdett, 1980).

Robert D. Duggan and Maureen A. Kelly, *The Christian Initiation of Children: Hope for the Future* (New York/Mahwah, NJ: Paulist Press, 1991).

James B. Dunning, *New Wine, New Wineskins: Exploring the RCIA* (Chicago/New York/Los Angeles: William H. Sadlier, 1981).

James B. Dunning, 'Saving parishes: community and conversion', *Church* 10.1 (Spring 1994), pp. 5–8.

Mircea Eliade, *The Sacred and the Profane* (New York: Harcourt, Brace and World, 1959).

Joseph Favazza, *The Order of Penitents: Historical Roots and Pastoral Future* (Collegeville, MN: Liturgical Press, 1989).

Austin Flannery OP (ed.), *Vatican Council II: The Conciliar and Post-Conciliar Documents* (Collegeville, MN: Liturgical Press, 1975).

Spiritus 134 (February 1994) (contains the papers of the international colloquium on the catechumenate which took place in Lyons, France, July 1993).

Thomas J. Talley, *The Origins of the Liturgical Year* (2nd edn; Collegeville, MN: Liturgical Press (orig. Pueblo Press), 1990).

It's about waiting 10

rediscovering a sacramental spirituality

Andrée Heaton

It has been remarked that the priestly or, more specifically, the eucharistic ministry is not to be reduced to that of the role of waiter. However, in a profound sense the image of the waiter can provide us with some significant insights into the nature of this distinctive Christian service.

The role of the waiter – or waitress – is not to compel or even to coax people to come to the restaurant but to welcome and serve them when they choose to do so, to the extent that this courtesy and attention to their needs may well be a decisive factor in determining whether or not they continue to frequent the restaurant, although it will only be one consideration amongst a number of others, notably the quality of the food and to what extent the restaurant really provides an ambiance in which, when the occasion arises, people can genuinely celebrate with friends and family, or a place where they can feel sufficiently at ease in order to communicate and share something of themselves with those with whom they wish to cultivate relationships at various levels of intimacy. Once the choice is made of the worthwhileness of the venue, the role of the waiter is not to determine who eats what and certainly not whether or not they may eat, but to draw their attention to what is offered and perhaps to guide them in their choice regarding what will be the most satisfying food and drink.

The waiter does not then, in any real sense, produce the food. She or he serves what is ready to eat, thanks to the creative skills of the chef. These in turn depend upon a complex network of services and forces of production and ultimately upon the availability of the earth's produce, whether abundant or meagre, rich in variety or limited, luxury food or a staple diet, costly or modestly priced. The task of the waiters is to serve the people who have chosen to eat in the restaurant where they are employed, but over and beyond this they may need to confront or be confronted by some pertinent questions about the choice of the restaurant in which they have decided to serve and to ask whose interests are served in so doing. These questions may be masked by short-term or purely personal considerations, including personal economic necessity, but they clearly relate to more far-reaching issues concerning the economic necessities of society at large and the global village in which we all need to eat, at whichever table we find ourselves. Waiters themselves may, of course, be the victims of economic and social injustice and it is a sobering thought that the 'service' industries, including catering concerns at both ends of the market, are often staffed by workers from poor countries who literally wait hungrily at the tables of the rich. On the other hand there may be an unpalatable collusion between the all too acquiescent waiter and a consumer society geared to the cultivation of appetites which ever more voraciously devour the fruits of the earth.

The link between these remarks on the familiar role of the waiter and reflection on the role of the eucharistic minister may now be seen as quite transparent.

The priest's task is not one of recruiting people to the eucharistic meal but of making them welcome when they choose to come, even though she or he may be a very significant agent in persuading them of the worthwhileness of so doing. The minister will almost certainly be influential in determining whether or not people feel it is worth continuing to gather for the Eucharist although they may decide to do so despite, rather than because of, the service they get. What is primarily incumbent on the celebrant is to create the space and atmosphere in which people may gather for an authentic celebration and the real sharing of lives and concerns which that entails. However, this is by no means the exclusive role of the one who presides over the assembly nor is it exclusive to that person. No amount of facilitating can force sharing if people are unwilling to engage in it, likewise the most uncongenial of environments may not impede interaction if people are really moved to communicate. Nevertheless in the eucharistic celebration the priest undoubtedly has a crucial part to play as enabler and animator since the liturgical celebrant is designated in a particular way to welcome those who gather round the eucharistic table and to cultivate their taste for the God-given nourishment of which the Lord, as the host, invites all to partake (Wisd 9:1–5, Isa 25:6, 55:1–3, Luke 14:15–24, Rev 19:9).

Given the importance habitually attached to the president of the eucharistic assembly we have to be on our guard against the persistence of mechanistic interpretations of the scholastic doctrine of transubstantiation[1] and we may still need to remind ourselves that the priest does not 'make' the Eucharist or 'make Christ present on the altar'. Such statements reflect an interventionist concept of God, a dualistic view of the relationship between the divine and the natural, created world and a perfunctory and elitist notion of the priest as the one who alone can bridge the gap between the two and inject the sacred into the profane. At the extreme this serves either to reduce the priest to a holy magician or to elevate the minister to the status of sole agent and executive of the divine absentee company director. The image of the priest as waiter, on the contrary, reminds us that his or her role is to prepare the table of the Lord and to serve the eucharistic meal which the Lord alone provides, albeit using human resources (Mark 6:30–44).[2]

These remarks rest on the fundamental Christian premiss that both creation and incarnation are the result of divine initiative because God is God. This principle is nowhere more apparent than in the theology and popular piety which has grown up around the figure of Mary, the virginal Servant of the Lord celebrated as one through whom 'the Almighty does great things' (Luke 1:49) and is made known as Emmanuel, God with us (Matt 1:23), really present in our midst. Despite the exaggerations and ambiguities surrounding the cult of the virgin mother, these beliefs rest on the fundamental conviction that no human beings could *make* God present in the world (Job 38 and 39); but more than requiring a recognition of the power of divine transcendence, this is an invitation to a celebration of liberating joy in divine immanence (Prov 8:30–31; Zeph 3:14–18; Luke 1:68–69, 78). The song of creation has long begun – we did not compose it but we are called to join in and to harmonize our lives with it. The Lord has long chosen to walk with us, we are invited to walk or indeed to dance with the God of our salvation, though we always have the privilege of refusing to do so (Matt 11:16–17, 19:21–22; Rev 3:20).

It is in this context of belief that the worshipping community reflects on and, more importantly, may experience the Eucharist as giving thanks for creation and giving thanks for new life.[3] But at what cost will there be new life? For whom will there be new life? Just as we take our supermarkets for granted despite a growing awareness of the 'politics of food' and the uncomfortable realization that there are scandalous inequalities in the availability of the earth's resources, how many priests and people gather for the eucharistic meal with only a token bidding prayer or maybe a second collection to remind them of the unpalatable reality that there are millions who are excluded from the world's table, let alone the table of the Lord? If as professed Christians we find ourselves only serving the needs of those who can afford to eat, maybe we should proclaim a fast whilst we attune our ears and our hearts to the cry of those who are really needy (Isa 1:11–17; James 2:15–17).

Perhaps this could give a fresh twist to our understanding of the priest as waiter – a good waiter will wait until all the guests have gathered and until the food is ready for each one of them before even beginning to serve. The role of the priest may be to remind people of this convention which, translated into the global context is no mere courtesy but a matter of sheer survival. Co-responsibility in this respect cannot be abdicated if worshippers are to pay more than lip service to their calling to go forth and build a better world[4] and if believers are to take seriously the ethical demands not only of the Jewish and Christian tradition (Isa 58:1–12; Matt 25:31–46) but the moral principles arising from our common humanity and propounded by all the great world faiths.

For all its richness, one of the great weaknesses of the image of the priest as waiter rests upon the fact that waiters are not included in the circle of diners, they are not a party to their communication or their celebration, they may not even speak their language and certainly do not share their lives or their reasons for being at the meal. Once the party has left the table, waiters are left alone to clear up and may never see them again. Sadly, a cynical view of the contemporary Church and its liturgy might tempt one to say that this is by no means an inaccurate portrayal of the way the priestly ministry is; but let us instead focus on what it may be. For this we need to move away from the image of the minister as the waiter at table and explore the broader notion of the ministry of waiting. This obliges us immediately to abandon the concentration on the figure of what one person – the waiter at table – does for a group (or even an individual), who sit down to have their needs attended to, to be waited upon.

In the biblical tradition, all are called to be 'waiters' in so far as all are called to serve the Lord and his people, with concern for the latter being the acid test of true devotion to the former (1 John 2:9–10, 3:17, 4:20–21). All this is so familiar as scarcely to merit reiterating, yet perhaps we do have to rehearse the old well-known stories of service in order to re-member the tradition which can so easily become dislocated (Luke 22:24–27; John 13:3–7). Certainly in the case of sacramental ministry there is a recurring risk of allowing religious and ritual formalities to stifle the Spirit so that we find ourselves in the killing fields of dry bones (Ezek 37:1–10) instead of pathways of the Spirit-filled servants of the living God (Ezek 37:11–14; Luke 1:76–79).

The question Christians have to ask themselves is the persistent biblical one: 'what must we do' in order to breathe fresh life into the old bones and for the Body of Christ to discover a fresh lease of life? It would seem that waiting is the key. In the biblical perspective the just person is one who 'waits on the Lord', significantly not first and foremost through 'active service' but through a profound attentiveness which requires a deep stillness and concentration on the focus of attention (Pss 46:10, 123:1–2, 130:5–6; Luke 10:38–42). Arguably in our achievement-orientated Western society we have paid too little attention to the importance of this prayer of stillness; all too often there is little or no space for silence and stillness in our sacramental liturgies. It is ironic that the monastic ideal has had such an influence on models of piety, not least priestly piety, in the Western Church, yet the fact that monasticism gives pride of place to contemplation has had so little effect on patterns of prayer and daily living for many devout Christians. Nevertheless the more frenetic our society becomes, the greater the need for wellsprings of contemplation which will help us to rediscover the primacy of waiting on the Lord.

Such waiting, however, is far from passive, and if it entails a retreat this is only ever temporary. Elijah retreats into the wilderness and encounters God in 'a sound of sheer silence' (1 Kings 19:12), only to be told 'Go, return on your way' – back to the very people he had wanted to avoid. Jesus withdraws to a quiet place to pray but never at the expense of serving the needs of the people who seek him (Mark 1:35–39). In the gospels the symbol of servants waiting for their Lord is presented as a model of discipleship but only if the waiters are alert (Matt 24:37–42) and the waiting is characterized by readiness for action (Matt 25:1–13; Luke 12:35–48).[5]

And for what should we be so ready to be galvanized into action? The well-worn answers will surely be that we must be ready for the service of the Lord and of one another – a statement that can mean everything or nothing but pious rhetoric. According to the New Testament it is evident that the disciples had to be ready for change: first the change within themselves – the metanoia – that the teaching of Jesus required (Mark 1:14–15; Col 3:5–17), but also change in their view of the society in which they found themselves, which was an inevitable consequence of refocusing their inner vision. Thus readiness to change from within inevitably led to the challenge to confront the need to change without, or at the very least readiness to cope within the inevitable confrontation between the vision inspired by the Kingdom and views which conflicted with it. This entailed the need to question whatever in the religious practice of the time no longer faithfully reflected the spirit of the covenant. Hence we see Jesus and later his disciples constantly challenging the religious establishment of their day (Matt 15:1–3; Mark 7). The study and interpretation of these narratives of conflict is clearly a specialized field, a survey of which goes beyond the scope of this chapter, which is not intended to endorse a simplistic view of Judaism in the first century CE as religiously decadent and the teaching of Jesus as totally 'new'.[6] Nevertheless, what emerges from a reading of the New Testament is the fact that Jesus, and subsequently his disciples, was frequently prepared to challenge the *status quo*, including the religious authorities of his time (John 2:13–20) and that he warned those who wished to follow him and serve the Kingdom that they must be prepared to suffer the consequences of daring to do this (Matt 10:14–20).

So much for the first century CE; what about the twenty-first? It would appear that those who today wish to wait on the Lord should draw inspiration and courage from the gospel tradition of religious disobedience to oppressive conventions (Mark 2:23–27, 3:1–5; Col 2:16, 20–22) and radical protest, in particular on behalf of those who are marginalized and exploited (Luke 4:18–24). This applies, of course, to all those who are abused and exploited in today's world. It also applies to those who are discriminated against or excluded in today's Church whether from the ecclesiastical community as a whole or from its assemblies for worship and its ministerial structures. Such exclusion is all the more debatable if it is based on what people by their very nature are (for example, female), or if they are simply exercising a universal right which Scripture itself sees as God-given (for example, the right to marry). If the Eucharist is 'about celebrating',[7] it is not about restricting the presidency of eucharistic celebrations to male celibates. If it is about making peace,[8] it is not about reinforcing the feelings of guilt of those who are already having to come to terms with the moral dilemma caused by a breakdown in relationships or the moral complexities of the situations in which they find themselves.

There is no doubt that the Christian community is impoverished by the exclusion or marginalization of people who fit uneasily into its established ministerial structures or whose lives do not fit into neat and simple categories of right and wrong. Yet to focus attention on these issues may seem like preoccupation with the conditions of service for the crew as the *Titanic* heads towards the iceberg. It may be argued that these are merely internal ecclesiastical concerns, not to say squabbles, which are relatively parochial and certainly of minor importance in comparison with the all too many glaring examples of injustice, the atrocities and the wanton destruction of the earth and its people confronting us beyond the ecclesiastical community and which, it could be argued, its members need more urgently to address. Nevertheless there are common principles at stake, namely commitment to justice, respect for the individual, acceptance of differences, complementarity and complexity. In serving neither category of need is the Christian absolved from attending to the other, for if we cannot care for the stranger (woman, divorcee, homosexual) in our midst how can we care for those further afield estranged by the sheer extent of their suffering? How can the Church credibly serve, let alone champion, the cause of justice and peace on the national and international scale if it fails to act justly towards its own members? It is difficult to see the ecclesiastical community as committed to human rights, the elimination of prejudice, and social development in society at large, if it is resistant to open debate, fresh insights and understanding within its own ranks, or even declares certain questions to be permanently removed from the agenda to be discussed, let alone implemented.[9]

There is 'a time for planting . . . a time for searching . . . a time for keeping silent . . . ' (Eccles 3:1–7). Likewise there is a time for waiting and being patient, but there is also a time for speaking out and for the waiting to be transposed into action in order that people may experience that 'the night is far gone' (Rom 1:3–12) and that '*now* is the day of salvation' (2 Cor 6:2).

NOTES

Biblical quotations are taken from the New Revised Standard Version of the Bible (Oxford: OUP, 1991).

1. A. Heron, *Table and Tradition* (Edinburgh: Handsel Press, 1983), pp. 93–102.
2. R. J. Leddgar, 'The Eucharistic Prayer and the gifts over which it is spoken' in K. Seasoltz (ed.), *Living Bread, Saving Cup* (Collegeville, MN: Liturgical Press, 1982).

3. Christiane Brusselmans, *We Celebrate the Eucharist* (Morristown, NJ: Silver Burdett, 1990), themes 6 and 7.
4. Ibid., theme 9.
5. W. H. Vanstone, *The Stature of Waiting* (London: Darton, Longman and Todd, 1982), chapter 7.
6. E. P. Sanders, *Jesus and Judaism* (London: SCM Press, 1984).
7. Christiane Brusselmans, op. cit., theme 2.
8. Ibid., theme 5.
9. P. Hebblethwaite, 'A theologian's dilemma on women priests', *The Tablet* (3 September 1994), p. 1114.

Part Two

Part Two

A coming to birth

empowering people in ministry

> From the beginning until now the entire creation, as we know, has been groaning in one great act of giving birth; and not only creation, but all of us who possess the first fruits of the Spirit; we too groan inwardly, as we wait for our bodies to be set free. (Rom 8:22–23)[1]

> The first creation finds its meaning and its summit in the new creation in Christ, the Splendour which surpasses that of the first creation.[2]

'THERE'S SOMETHING HAPPENING in the Church and to the Church, though I'm not quite sure what it is.' How often have you heard such a statement since the Second Vatican Council? How does it leave you feeling? For some there is a sense of fear – a fear of the unknown, or of something precious being lost; for others there is a sense of excitement, a need to be changing and re-focusing, for taking responsibility and for coming to birth.

It reminds me of the Church as Mother, who as a woman bringing a child to birth does not wait passively, but waits creatively, as she forms within her womb this new creation. The shaping of any new life is a slow, gradual process, one which takes place in the darkness of the unknown. This calls for a trust – a trust in God's unending loving care, working in everyone and through everything. That we are, as individuals or communities, part of this unfolding plan places us in a position of wonder and awe, together with a deep sense of co-responsibility as co-creators.

115

This new birth was consequent on the renewed sacramental theology of Vatican II. It comprehended a new understanding of Church as the Pilgrim People of God and an appreciation of baptism as itself constituting a call to ministry. But the very working out of this theology pushed developments further, and brought about a changed consciousness, which was influenced by other factors, including women's spirituality.

In 'A coming to birth' I endeavour to trace a few simple ways in which I see signs of growth and maturity taking shape in the Church, particularly in the area of empowering people for ministry. The first is from my own experience as an apostolic religious sister, the second from my experience as a member of a parish community.

Because of circumstances beyond our control – the re-organization of schools, the deaths and ageing of members of the Congregation – the large convent I lived in was closed and a small house for two was opened. This gave me an opportunity to acquire an interest in gardening, to be in touch with the soil, sowing seeds, pruning, making compost and waiting for new growth and eventful fruitfulness. This experience named for me the pruning and slow growth that we religious women are being called to at the present moment in our history. Due to lack of vocations and falling numbers we began to ask questions. The asking of questions about our way of life was the necessary 'groaning' we had to endure before we emerged from the darkness. It was at this time of questioning that we did not look outside ourselves for solutions but touched into the experience of the apostles who were told to 'wait for what the Father had promised' (Acts 1:4). Like the apostles we too asked the Lord: 'Lord, has the time come? Are you going to restore the kingdom to Israel?' He replied: 'It is not for you to know times or dates that the Father has decided by his own authority, but *you will receive power* when the Holy Spirit comes upon you and then you will be my witness . . . ' (Acts 1:6–8).

This moment was the beginning of a recognition that we had an 'authority', a 'power' within us, both as individuals and as a congregation. This power needed to be 'set free' – we needed to be 'set free'. The congregation needed to empower each of us to stand in the 'truth of our own integrity' and to discover that our true freedom comes from the liberation that Christ gives. We had a choice to make – either to die out gracefully or take the challenge of refounding religious life. The choice to refound meant that we had to learn to work together, to clarify our vision, to come to a new appreciation of the giftedness of the other, and to trust one another and ourselves. We had to take ownership for ourselves and our congregation . . . we were truly becoming women.

There was the gradual letting go of our congregational habit and logo – naturally so precious to many sisters. The remodelling of the logo was symbolic. Instead of a figureless ebony cross on a coffin-shaped, starched, guimpe, we now, through a long process of discernment and consultation, have a small, figureless cross at the centre of a womb-shaped silver pendant. This womb-shaped pendant symbolizes our decision to bring to birth a new way of living and being, with Christ at the centre. We recognize anew the call to be 'in Christ' and that through our response, rooted in our baptismal vocation, we have the potential to become 'a new creation in him'. This calls for us to remain buried in the darkness of the womb waiting for the birth of our new true selves. 'Unless a grain of wheat falls on the ground and dies it remains only a single grain. But if it dies, it yields a rich harvest' (John 12:24).

Chaos or Creation speaks of the birth process of each of us when we are called through deeper interiority and receptivity to bring forth our own child.[3] When our time comes there is indeed a wrenching pain as an era of life ends and a period of disorientation and confusion ensues prior to bringing forth the authentic personality – Paul's 'hidden self'.

For all of us can surely identify with the wrenching pain and the period of disorientation and confusion. Will it ever end? Whilst we continue to struggle it is fascinating to witness the emergence and blossoming of a variety of ministries in the Church. Many of these ministries formerly belonged only to the ordained priesthood or to the religious life. These ministeries are constantly being awakened and affirmed within the local parish community. The significance of the Synod on the Vocation and Mission of the Lay Faithful 'might well consist in this call of the Lord which is addressed to everyone, yet in a particular way to the lay faithful, both women and men'.[4] It is described in the Synod response as a

> Christian newness of life – a sense of Church communion, the gift of the Spirit, that urges our generous and free response which will bring forth as its precious fruit the continuing value of the rich variety of vocations and conditions of life, of charisms, ministries, works and responsibilities.[5]

In our letting go we, in some hidden way, are bringing forth the 'new child' of lay ministry. 'A woman in childbirth suffers, because her time has come: but when she has given birth to the child, she forgets the suffering in her joy that a child has been born into the world' (John 16:21).

We recognize that the Spirit who works in surprising ways is moving the Church into the age of the laity, empowering people in different ways for ministry. This empowerment is leading to a discovery of a whole new way of life, an understanding of the universal call to holiness and a spirituality of living the Gospel each moment of our lives. Alongside this is a recognition of the call to come before God as a community, and not merely as individuals. It is often in weakness and brokenness that the Spirit can operate fruitfully. This is the Christian movement from crucifixion to resurrection.

I would now like to illustrate this movement in tracing the story of Maggie's call to ministry, and not only her coming 'to newness of life', but the impact on her parish community. It was obvious the times we spoke to Maggie at church that she was in quiet desperation, struggling to make sense of her life as wife and mother of two young, demanding children aged five and six. Her 'inward groanings' were expressed in anger against her husband, who was working long hours away from home, and against her two boys as they became increasingly uncontrollable, especially during Sunday Eucharist. Maggie's appearance began to reflect her frustration, her lack of self-values and self-esteem. Here was a woman, gifted with intelligence and deep faith, 'dying' before our very eyes, yearning to be 'set free'.

One Sunday the fuse blew. The boys had been intolerable at Mass. 'Why doesn't *the Church* do something for them?' she shrieked. Her desperation was echoed by many of the parents as they shared their stories of feelings of inadequacy and anger. Their frustrated 'Why doesn't the Church?' gradually softened until it became: 'Why don't we? – after all, *we* are the Church!' Within a few weeks these parents set about claiming their responsibilities in the parish community by ensuring that the children were involved in their own Liturgy of the Word at Sunday Eucharist. Their recognition of '*we* are the Church' was a moment of gift to our parish community. This was a first small step in a profound process of change that is continually bringing new life to the parish. In fact it is a new way of being Church. No longer behaving like children waiting for help to come from above – but behaving as adults who recognize a need, and creatively respond to it. This is truly accepting the call to share in Christ's mission – rooted in our baptismal vocation of 'not only belonging to the Church, but of being Church'.[6]

These parents arranged to meet together on a weekly basis to prepare for the children's Liturgy. In reading the Word and reflecting on it, in order to ensure it echoed the children's own lived experience, the adults discovered something new and powerful for themselves. Week by week they were being immersed in the Scriptures and began to recognize a power at work within themselves, their families and the wider parish community.

> For in these books [the Scriptures] God the Father meets his children lovingly and speaks with them. The force and power in the word of God is so strong that it gives support and energy to the Church; is strength of faith for the faithful, is food for the soul, is the everlasting source of spiritual life.[7]

For most of these parents this was the first time that they had prayed the Scripture or engaged in any form of faith-sharing. It touched a deep hunger within them which they were able to name. It was the beginning of discovering a little of their spirituality as lay people in the Church. Some of the group enrolled in Bible study classes, others sought spiritual direction or retreat opportunities. They all recognized the need for personal renewal in order to minister to the children and to one another.

A bonding was taking place. They were, unknown to themselves, being formed into a small Christian community, rooted in and nourished on the Word, with the challenge to become more fully the Body of Christ:

> In virtue of their rebirth in Christ there exists among all Christ's faithful a true equality with regard to dignity and the activity whereby all co-operate in the building up of the Body of Christ in accord with each one's own condition and function.[8]

Friendships blossomed, barbecues, parish walks and discos were organized so that a network of support was gradually formed. The effect of this permeated into their own families and homes. These became places of healing and forgiveness, of love and support – truly becoming the 'domestic church'.

> The family has received from God its mission to be the first and vital cell of society. It will fulfil this mission if it shows itself to be the domestic sanctuary of the Church through mutual affection of its members and the common prayer they offer to God if the family is

caught up in the liturgical worship of the Church, and if it provides active hospitality and promotes justice and other good works for the service of all in need.

In this way they responded to the call to: 'allow the newness and the power of the gospel to shine out every day in their family and social life, as well as to express patiently and courageously in the contradictions of the present age their hope of future glory'.[10]

Building on the hospitality offered by different families in the parish, there emerged small groups of people who began to share the hopes and fears, joys and sufferings of life. From the initial greeting, 'Hello, how are you?', came a new way of meeting people where they were: 'How are *you*? How are you coping at the moment?' A ministry of like-to-like developed with support for bereaved, separated and divorced, single parents, alcoholics etc. People began to recognize the pain and the struggle within each other and tapped into the vast reservoir of experience of life's daily living. It was in these moments of sharing and of listening that a discovery was made of God's presence in the chaos of our lives.

> Often I look at the compost and marvel at its mystery. As year after year I meditate on it, increasingly it opens up its secret. It unfolds the reality of life, death and resurrection at the heart of creation's mystery. Everywhere it is proclaimed: as a seed buried in the ground sprouts a tree; as leaves in the forest decay into soft earth; as a caterpillar becomes a butterfly; and as an infant is released from the body of a woman. Something always gives way, dies, so it appears, for new life to emerge. To return to the image of the compost, bacteria generate heat and energy for its transformation. Similarly, the Spirit of God, like a divine fire, energizes us in our messiness that we too might realize transformation and the fullness of our potential. Difficult experiences provide the stuff of inner transformation.[11]

This is also beautifully expressed:

> Only in the unfolding of the history of our lives is the eternal plan of God revealed to each one of us. It is a gradual process, one that happens day by day. Every area of our lives, as different as they are, enters into the plan of God who desires that these very areas be the places where the love of Christ is revealed and realized for both the glory of the Father and the services of others.[12]

One of the fruits, the recognition of the sacredness of our lives, was a blessed moment resulting in a need within us of giving thanks. The Sunday Eucharist became the highlight of the week. We celebrated being the Body of Christ, called in our brokenness to minister to one another. We rejoiced in being nourished by the Body and Blood of Christ, in being ministered to by the community, the Body of Christ.

Our horizons are naturally being extended through the challenge of the Eucharist. The call to work for justice, peace, the equality and dignity of all people, and for the care of the environment is being heard. The establishment of a Parish Pastoral Team is just the first small step for us. We recognize that collaborative ministry is the way forward, knowing that what we do together would be impossible for us to do alone. We do have many more questions than solutions, but we know that we now have a 'confidence' in our own giftedness, and 'authority' within us, a 'power' and an 'energy' which can no longer be tamed or subdued. For it is the power of the risen Lord Jesus at work within us, waiting to be set free. To bring about the transformation of humanity our task now is to empower others to be part of this transformation. We can do this by engaging them in the decision-making that affects their lives and society at large. 'There is no new humanity unless there are new persons renewed by baptism.'[13] By empowering people we are inviting them to be involved in a revolutionary task, that of bringing the Church to birth for a new millennium. 'A religious vision for the third millenium' complements this thinking: 'Religious futurists perceive the task of religion in the 21st century to be that of a midwife who can facilitate the birth of a new global community.'[14]

The difficulties encountered in bringing about this vision must not be underestimated. Recently a friend started his homily at a wedding: 'No contraception, no abortion, no divorce – the Catholic Church's teaching on marriage – so we are told by the media.' He continued: 'It's a very destructive and negative approach to a universal and fundamental state of life ... it should make us question whether such a negative view is an accurate reflection of what the Church teaches about marriage.'

Maybe we need to be aware of such negative and destructive attitudes regarding our new way of being Church. Reflection is vital. Are we in danger of practising contraception in the area of preventing the seeds of new life taking root in the lay faithful called to ministry? Are we in danger of aborting new growth in case our position is threatened and 'they become too powerful'? Are there times when we contemplate divorce, making decisions to go it alone or with excuses that people do not want this responsibility? Bringing about the vision calls for a new style of leadership, a leadership which will be enhanced and enriched by the contribution of women in particular, who have experienced the pain and pressures of the letting go involved in bringing forth new life.

Christiane Brusselmans, a single laywoman, combined the qualities of both mother and midwife in her struggle to be true to that creative power within her. As mother, Christiane's openness and receptivity conceived a vision of Church. In bringing this vision to birth she was called to empty herself. In her brokenness she brought forth new life for so many people within the Church. As midwife, Christiane has handed over to us the responsibility of nurturing and forming this new creation. In receiving this gift may we grow to full maturity in Christ and in the Church through the transforming power of the Spirit, who calls us to ministry.

> There, in that other world, what waits for me?
> What shall I find after that other birth?
> No stormy, tossing, foaming, smiling sea,
> But a new earth.
>
> No sun, to mark the changing of the day.
> No slow, soft falling of the alternate night.
> No moon, no star, no light upon my way,
> Only the light.
>
> No grey cathedral, wide and wondrous fair,
> That I may tread where all my fathers trod.
> Nay, nay, my soul, no house of God is there,
> But only God.[15]

NOTES

1. Biblical quotations are from the Jerusalem Bible (London: Darton, Longman and Todd, 1966).
2. *Catechism of the Catholic Church* (London: Geoffrey Chapman, 1994), no. 349.
3. L. Patrick Carroll and Catherine Marie Dyckman, *Chaos or Creation: Spirituality in Mid-Life* (New York: Paulist Press, 1986), p. 303.
4. *Christifideles Laici* (London: CTS, 1988; Do. 589), 64.

5. Ibid.
6. Ibid., 9.
7. *This Is Divine Revelation: Simplification of the Constitution* Dei Verbum (Pinner: Grail Publications, 1986), 21.
8. *Catechism of the Catholic Church*, no. 872.
9. 'Decree on the Apostolate of the Laity' in W. M. Abbott SJ (ed.), *Documents of Vatican II* (London: Geoffrey Chapman, 1967), 11.
10. *Christifideles Laici*, 14.
11. Vilma Seelaus, 'Fragmentation and divine transformation: meditation on a compost heap', *The Way* (October 1988), no. 4.
12. *Christifideles Laici*, 59.
13. *Evangelii Nuntiandi* (London: CTS; Do. 5312, 1976), 18.
14. Earl Brewer, 'A religious vision for the third millenium', *The Futurist* (1988) (Bethesda, MD: The World Future Society).
15. Mary Coleridge, 'There' in *Poems and Prayers* (Oxford: Lion Publications, 1981), p. 80.

Collaborative ministry – an obstinate hope

12

reflections on an experience of Church

ANGELA M. LAWRENCE

THOMAS MERTON wrote that a faith that has to be defended every day of the week isn't worth a penny. Faith has to be experienced and lived. Out of the work and spirit of Vatican II there flowed a theological hope that the Gospel could continue to be lived and proclaimed to a humankind rich in its diversity. The radical call of the Gospel is for each one of us as individuals, for the local faith community and the Church as the universal family. For the Gospel to become alive each one of us, each community, the Church itself, has to experience the depths of conversion of the call to prayer, service and social justice.

In this essay I reflect upon the impact of Vatican II on the life of one diocese through my experience of being actively involved in adult education. It is an account of an attempt at a lived theology and what that means in human terms within the institutional Church – times for rejoicing, times for mourning. Hope and vision confronted by frustration, pain and anger.

In the midst of it all there exists a belief in and commitment to the spirit and living out of collaborative ministry: a belief that it is only in our deep respect for each other's unique gifts and ministries that we have any hope of a way forward in the Church. One is reminded of the stark contrast between being alive to the heart of the 'Good News' and the counter-experience of struggling with one's faith through 'the desert' and recognizing how people can be marginalized. Yet our stories in the telling reflect a theology lived out of a Gospel that integrates our hopes and fears, our sense of brokenness and healing. It was Oscar Romero who reassured his people by telling them: 'If they murder me do not worry ... After all,

all they are doing is killing a bishop. But the Church will not die for the Church is the people of God.'

Ten years ago in the diocese of Arundel and Brighton, as in many parts of the UK, the Vatican II vision of Church as the pilgrim People of God was gradually emerging. A new dawn was touching diocesan horizons and those who turned to welcome it rejoiced in the light of its promise. The bishop (whose heraldic motto was *Gaudium et Spes*) proclaimed the Church with joy and hope as a communion of small communities where individuals might experience, in the reality of daily living, fellowship with God and with one another in and through the life-giving Spirit. However, in those early days of gradual change in the ecclesial milieu, the deeply rooted institutional model continued to prevail in practice. This was not altogether surprising, given the paucity of preparation of both clergy and laity towards an understanding and appreciation of the renewed vision of Church presented by the Council some twenty years earlier. Tensions were inevitable, rumblings surfaced and found voice, challenging growth and development not least where programmes of adult formation began to gather momentum.

Several years after *Catechesi Tradendae* the reality of systematic, integrated catechesis remained fairly minimal. For generations the accent had been on instruction, on acquiring knowledge about the faith rather than on dialogue and faith-sharing within a faith community. Emerging programmes of adult religious education tended to follow familiar, didactic patterns: lectures concerned with imparting maximum information to maximize 'audiences' and not always paying sufficient attention to life experience, to the building of relationships (essential to creating a sense of Church), to outreach and evangelization. A tendency remained towards compartmentalization both of knowledge and of individuals. Looking back over the intervening years, I imagine this was a scene familiar to many of us as the Spirit summoned up the winds of change and breathed the beginnings of new life into our experience of Church.

Against this background one of the areas in which the emerging model of Church began to take root was in those parishes engaged in the so-called 'new' sacramental programmes, especially the preparation for first communion, in which the entire parish community was encouraged to take part, surfacing a variety of hitherto unheard-of ministries. Inspired by two visits of Christiane Brusselmans to the diocese, her nine-month programme 'We Celebrate the Eucharist', based on the RCIA, was adopted by a growing number of parishes. At grassroots level this presented an opportunity for home, school and parish to work together, each playing their unique role of contributing their own gifts and skills to community-based catechesis. At first, the schools did not always find it easy to adjust to this change. Understandably, some felt a sense of rejection. Until that time, had not the parish primary school (i.e., the 'First Communion teacher') carried through most, if not all, of the preparation for the sacrament? The parents too felt threatened. How could they possibly prepare their own children? Had that not always been the responsibility of the school? After all, they were not teachers . . . They were only parents!

Time, patience and sensitive catechesis rooted in sound theology were needed if all parties were to grow in an understanding of what it means to *be* Church (rather than to 'go to' church). The first step was to bring together the various groups (frequently for the first time), enabling them to meet one another, listen to each other, share doubts, hopes, concerns and dreams – to share their stories. In the sharing, and in reflection on the Word, speaking within the sharing, came an awareness of travelling together, each with his/her own strengths and frailties, yet supporting one another in what was gradually being recognized as a life-long journey of faith. Two of the observations frequently expressed by parents at that time: 'It's such a relief to know I'm not meant to have arrived yet! I don't have to have it all sewn up . . . ' and 'We're not expected to go it alone!' Both were spoken with a sense of real joy and freedom. People were beginning to experience what it means to be Church, to be part of the pilgrim People of God. As Avery Dulles SJ observes in his commentary on the Church as Mystical Communion: 'People find the meaning of their lives not in terms of such institutions but in terms of the informal, the personal, the communal. They long for a community which, in spite of all the conflicts built into modern society, can open up loving communication. The Church, if it can perform this function, will be enthusiastically welcomed.'[1]

Encouraged by their first steps into community-based catechesis, a number of parishes went on to implement Christiane's similar programme of preparation for the sacrament of reconciliation. Interest was shown in a more relevant catechesis for baptism. At the same time a community catechesis for teenage confirmation candidates was developing across the diocese and several parishes were beginning the RCIA. The harvest was indeed ripe, but as usual the labourers were few. It was obvious that there was an urgent need for trained catechists to work at local level, enabling the many emerging areas of catechesis to be as fruitful as possible.

Responding to this need, the diocesan education team offered a one-year, part-time course for leading catechists. Deans were encouraged by the bishop to send two likely candidates from each of the twelve deaneries. Trained to train others in their local areas, they were to provide a network of resource across the diocese as well as a support group within their own number. At the end of the year, having qualified for a diocesan certificate, they were commissioned by the bishop for their ministry. One of the prime, perceived values of the course linked learning to relating; growth in knowledge and pastoral skills within a community context in which faith and experience were shared, prayed and celebrated. The fruitful partnership of priests and laypeople within the education team was seen as a powerful witness to collaboration in ministry.

It was out of a process of evaluation, looking to the future development of this initial course, that the adult Christian education course 'Sharing Our Story' was conceived. The title was inspired by, and intended to reflect the theme of, the then recently published book by Fr Patrick Purnell SJ: *Our Faith Story: Its Telling and Its Sharing.*[2] This seminal work for the National Project in Religious Education sponsored by the hierarchy for the homes, schools and parishes in England and Wales was welcomed as the foundation book for the new course. As a result of recommendations from the leading catechists, 'Sharing Our Story' (or 'SOS' as it was soon to become known) was to extend over two years, part time. Experience had taught the need for time and space in which to assimilate new ideas, create community and grow in understanding, appreciation and commitment to a Vatican II Church. With the intention of fostering the unification of like-minded people (as well as the best use of limited resources) it was decided to combine the Teachers' RE Certificate course with SOS.

While attention had been given to maintaining the quality of academic standards, it was intended from the beginning that SOS would have a significant community dimension with opportunities for mutual enrichment, sharing and support. If our aim was to serve a post-Vatican II Church in its rediscovery of community rooted in the Gospel, then we could do no less than try to live that model ourselves. In moving towards that aim our immediate concern was with formation for ministry in the market place of work and leisure, as well as in the homes, schools and parishes of the diocese. Formation involves something much broader and wider than following a particular series of lectures – no matter how excellent they may be. Dr Clare Watkins, course director for the London-based Education for Parish Service, from her experience in lay training and education, writes:

> Formation for ministry is rarely, if ever, a matter of 'going on a course'. Rather, it is about a more general learning experience in which the resources of the person's experiences and faith are brought into critical relation with the wide variety of theological approaches and sources – Scripture, doctrine, liturgy, pastoral skills. It is only in such a wide-ranging *formation* that a properly em-powered lay ministry can begin to develop, empowered both by an increased expertise and an authentic spiritual formation.[3]

While there have in recent years been encouraging signs of growth in the area of formation for ministry, here in the UK we still have a long way to go in recognizing and resourcing what is fast becoming a matter of urgency.

Some thirty people eventually committed themselves to the first full SOS course, fairly evenly divided between those seeking the Teachers' RE Certificate and those hoping to gain a diocesan qualification. Teachers were supported by their schools and course fees subsidized by their local education authorities. Others required written support for their applica-tion from their parish priest or dean, indicating the likelihood of further opportunity for leadership in the Church. The bishop asked that parishes and deaneries consider subsidizing applicants, especially for the diocesan certificate.

In those days the concept of collaboration in ministry remained, to a great extent, locked safely away in the realms of theory – while joint formation for that ministry was, with few exceptions, uncharted territory. Ten years on, we can all look back and be thankful for the fruitful growth that has since taken place in this vital area of a post-Vatican II Church. But few of us can afford to be complacent. At a stage when, in our own country, people are beginning to experience the reality of the *priestless parish*, progress is patchy: wondrously transforming in some places, hardly begun in others. One senses a holy impatience with the slow dismantling of those structures which served the Church in a bygone age, but now are obstacles to proclaiming the Gospel in the less structured, pluralistic society of today.

From the beginning, there was the will on the course to build a real sense of community, to play an active role in a diocese taking its first steps towards becoming a communion of small communities. Frequently endorsed was the value of a whole day together, providing time to unwind (many travelled long distances) and space for reflection, exchange of ideas and experience, a shared meal and communal prayer. At the end of each day groups of students took their turn at creating a liturgy arising out of the day's experience. Each unit (of some several weeks) concluded with a celebration of Eucharist and 'party' supper. A growing sense of community, of genuine companionship, was greatly enhanced by three residential weekends which offered opportunities for liturgy to be lived and celebrated.

Although people were scarcely aware of it at the time, in retrospect these gatherings came to manifest several of the characteristics of basic Christian communities in their focus on the Word, mutual sharing and support, pastoral outreach and movement towards an ever-widening network of circles across the diocese. 'The basic Christian community is the first and fundamental ecclesial nucleus ... It is the initial cell of the ecclesial structure.'[4] In the various gatherings there developed a tangible awareness of the essential focus of community: 'Where two or three are gathered in my name, there I am in the midst of them' (Matt 18:20).

Out of this experience of community sprang a natural facility for storytelling. As we came to a deeper appreciation of our unique place in the People of God, sharing the journey not only with fellow pilgrims today, but also with all those who have gone before us signed with the sign of faith, there came a recognition and owning of one's story and a valuing of each one's story in the light of the timeless story of God's love constantly at work amongst his people. 'We are back into a community of stories and storytellers. In interpreting our traditional stories of God we find out who we are and what we must do. In telling the stories of God we ourselves are told.'[5] Luke 24:13–35 became the Scripture touchstone of the course, returned to time and again in reflection and celebration. The Emmaus story reflected so much of our experience – a pilgrimage of faith and doubts, of searching, losing and finding again, hearts burning within us as we come to recognize in our own stories, in word and in bread broken and shared, the risen Christ journeying with us.

Where the pastoral dimension had always been recognized as a vital element throughout the course, specific attention was given to an understanding of discipleship, to mission and evangelization in the unit devoted to Formation for Ministry. A sound grounding in the theology of ministry was followed by an explanation of the various ministries as ways in which we are today called through baptism to serve the Church in the world. In order that ideas might be rooted in practice, all the diocesan commissions were invited to take part, meeting the students and sharing with them the essence of their own particular areas of ministry. By opening up lines of communication and putting these people in touch with one another, the aim was to develop a fruitful partnership at local level in the work for Christian unity, justice and peace, youth, marriage and family life, liturgical formation. Ideally, every deanery and parish would eventually have a representative for each of these areas of ministry working together with the various commissions. Exciting and ambitious though it may have been, the idea was not new. Rather, it was an attempt to contribute to a more fruitful implementation of the existing ground plan for communication and collaboration throughout the diocese, a rooting of the vision of Church as family. Ten years on, through several less than successful attempts and more than one return to the drawing board, the search continues for an effective strategy for collaborative ministry which will win the commitment of both clergy and laity. Structures no longer relevant can dull the ear to the prophetic call.

What happened? Those who had, from the beginning, been supported by their parishes were warmly welcomed, their ministry explained to the parish community and sometimes endorsed by a further commissioning witnessed by their local community. Thus, they were enabled to strengthen, enrich and extend the existing areas of catechesis and formation as well as initiate new projects (e.g. RCIA). A significant number moved into leadership roles in parish, deanery and diocese. They continued to come together two or three times a year for a day's reunion at the Education Centre. These were powerful occasions for the bonding and sustaining of community, for evaluation of pastoral experience leading into future planning; a time for affirmation and encouragement, for the healing of hurts and the supporting of those in difficult pastoral situations.

The existing framework for adult formation throughout the diocese received a great boost when a number from SOS joined the ranks of the dozen (voluntary) adult formation co-ordinators, each one representing one of the twelve deaneries. The co-ordinator met once or twice a term with the adult formation representatives from the parishes of his or her deanery so that together they might discern local needs in adult Christian education and plan an appropriate response. One of the most successful deaneries was unique in that the co-ordination was shared in a recognized partnership between a priest and a laywoman. All twelve deanery co-ordinators then came together once a term at the Diocesan Education Centre when, in a spirit of friendship, they shared their experiences in the field – so that together they were able to evaluate past events and plan future projects. This was an enormous leap in assessing current educational priorities and in formulating a co-ordinated response at the levels of parish, deanery and diocese.

All, however, was not sweetness and light. We know that no pilgrim road is for long devoid of stumbling blocks and pitfalls. The years of SOS were not without their difficulties. Mingled with the joy and enthusiasm there was also pain and frustration. While some members of the clergy could not have been more supportive and encouraging, there were those who were not entirely noted for their interest and support. This was not always due to a lack of good will, but sometimes to a lack of understanding. From the beginning, commitment to 'priests and people together' had been the underpinning of SOS and of adult formation throughout the diocese. In our naïvety we had imagined that the theology – the common sense of collaboration – would be welcomed. This was not always so. For generations the laity had known little other than a subservient role. Many were now hesitant to take on responsibility in a Church whose changes they did not always understand. Those who were willing to play a more active role were not always regarded without suspicion. And what forma-tion had the clergy received to prepare them for collaboration in ministry – a partnership essential to the rooting and maintaining of Church as the People of God? Not everyone has the natural ability to relate to, and work with, others, but there are skills which can be taught and learned. What access had the clergy had to such training?

Out of this reality, individuals who had willingly devoted much time and energy to meet the demands of the SOS course now found it more than a little difficult to find an opening in their own parishes. Their ministry was not understood and therefore not recognized. At the general gatherings of leading catechists a motivating frustration felt by the majority found voice. What value did their hard work, certificate and the bishop's commissioning have if these were not appreciated at local level? What price all the theory and documentation relating to lay involvement? As well as general frustration, individual stories told of personal hurt, rejection and marginalization. It was then that healing was found in the ministering to one another, strength in genuine affirmation and support, inspiration in prayer, especially in reflection on the Scriptures and renewed joy and resolution in celebration together. Reflection on their own experience in the light of the Church's pilgrimage down the ages enabled them to accept the inevitable tensions experienced by the Church at this stage of the journey. Patience, perseverance and a lot of love were essential if attitudes were to change and people be enabled to grow into a post-Vatican II vision of Church. Meanwhile, anything that might authentically move the process on from 'dead slow' would be more than welcome.

When, therefore, RENEW (a programme for parish renewal) was introduced into the diocese it was warmly received by all who recognized it as a means of breathing new life into parish roots. The choice was made, however, to go for a completely new and separate programme of minister-ial formation essential to the implementation of RENEW. Obviously there were advantages in opting for this choice, namely, that of a new beginning, new people, new faces. Those who had been somewhat slow in responding to previous pastoral initiatives were now offered the chance of a fresh start. However, this did not serve to minimize the sense of rejection and marginalization on the part of those who had for some time now 'borne the heat of the day' in the field of lay formation, including SOS and the leading catechists who at first appeared to have no contribution to make to the new project.

It was a time for the testing of hearts, a focusing on priorities, recogniz-ing the cost as well as the joy of discipleship. When all is said and done, what does discipleship really mean? What is it for? In searching for answers that would speak to the immediacy of the situation, there came a certain 'letting go', a learning to trust. Amongst other things, the realization that no matter how affectionately and loyally one regards the home territory of the local church, the Kingdom of God is greater than any diocese and, of course, greater than them all. First and last, it was the Kingdom that mattered. That is where the priority lies. The Church itself is a structure for the journey, not the final destination. It is part of the society which it is striving to renew in the light of Gospel values.

The spirit of vitality that had characterized SOS continued to operate across the diocese and beyond as its members moved into new ministries and forged new communities while retaining links with the old. In addition to the ministries now found in most parishes, there are those who have since trained as prayer guides, spiritual directors, bereavement coun-sellors. One is chairperson of the diocesan pastoral council – a key post in the development of collaborative ministry. Christiane Brusselmans once told me that she realized her vocation in the people she taught, in the midst of those with whom the Word was broken, celebrated and shared. I now know what she meant.

It has been said that SOS was ahead of its time. Perhaps it was. If so, that was part of its prophetic ministry, preparing the way, laying foundations for greater things to come. The students used to remark jokingly that John the Baptist should be their special patron – they so often felt like voices crying in the wilderness. John was called to prepare the way, aware that in so doing, 'He must increase, I must decrease' (John 3:30). All of us have, at some time, to experience the paradox that the seeds we have sown must die if they are to bear an abundance of fruit, fruit we had never dreamed of, fruit that will last (John 12:24). It is a painful, though necessary, stage of the journey, but it leads to resurrection, to new life in the here and now.

A collaborative model of ministry calls for a radical analysis of Church structures, challenging *all* those involved to move forward. Clericalism, as opposed (literally opposed) to priesthood, is one of the great obstacles requiring transformation. Impeded by residual shackles of an old, institutional model, there is as yet little freedom to enjoy the benefits of the new. How many of our priests can count on members of a parish team, fully trained and reasonably remunerated, enabling them to work with their priests, full or part time, in serving the needs of their community? This, it would seem, is where the crunch comes in collaborative ministry. What are we doing to bring about a relevant, effective and *joint* formation of clergy and laity for the partnership in ministry to which we are being called? Talent, skill and generosity are not lacking. A radical re-thinking of priorities is required. Recent experience has taught us that limited financial resources cannot adequately serve both an old and new model of Church. We cannot put new wine into old wine skins. If the Church of tomorrow (and tomorrow is dawning) is to address the general needs of our whole culture, then a change of attitude is called for and the practicalities of long-term planning need to start now.

While recent years have seen more laypeople involved in the decision-making process in their own parishes, this is seldom the case at diocesan level. Advisory and consultation status is not sufficient and only undermines efforts towards real collaboration. In one of the papers commissioned by the RC bishops for their special period of reflection last autumn, Clifford Longley suggested a new strategy for the Catholic

Church in England and Wales. While recognizing the authentic limits to democracy in both the Church and society, he draws attention to the role of the laity in an increasingly democratized society:

> A hierarchical Church which operates in a democratic society will have to create every possible opportunity for participation and sharing responsibility . . . Renewed emphasis on the vocation of the laity may be desirable for the needs of the Church itself. But for the engagement of the Church with society when society is a democracy, that lay vocation is completely essential and there is no alternative.[6]

Participation and sharing of responsibility can hardly happen in isolation. They are the fruits of community, energized by the Spirit. But have we in these islands yet learned to take community seriously? Do we recognize it as an essential pastoral task in the mission of the Church today? Or is it still regarded in many instances as something peripheral, a low-key, optional extra?

At the recent synod of African bishops the centrality of community was frequently emphasized, together with that partnership in ministry which is born out of community, nourished and sustained by it. Bishop Francisco Jodo Silota of Chimoio in Mozambique made the point that any pastoral strategy which omitted small Christian communities would be creating a Church without a future. Archbishop Anthony Mayola of Tanzania suggested that the work of the laity in evangelization, including the building up of small Christian communities, was being hindered by what he called the ingrained institutional and hierarchical model of the Church and pre-Vatican II mentality. He considered this a great obstacle to the ministries of the laity.[7] Is this a picture limited to a distant continent? Or do we find parallels within our own, local church?

The creation and sustaining of genuine community cannot appear from nowhere, plucked as it were out of the blue. It could be that some of us need to develop those inter-personal skills essential to the building of real community. When the need for such skills is ignored, when they are not considered important, then the generating of community becomes very difficult and people tend to give up the struggle. We come back again to the need for effective formation of all within the Church. Out of the experience of the post-Vatican II years, it is becoming increasingly apparent that those qualities usually associated with the female have a particular contribution to make in the building of community. As far back as 1980, the bishops of England and Wales in their response to the National Pastoral Congress in Liverpool valued the gifts of women in the Church with these words:

> Your particular gift for relationships makes you invaluable in any attempt to create communities. We believe the time is overdue for more positive attitudes about your participation in the life of the Church . . . Our appeal is that each of you individually will feel able to use to the full your gifts, your skills and your knowledge in the life and service of the Church. Traditional attitudes towards women and your role may have to be changed, we ourselves and our clergy may have to be persuaded of our insensitivity and our assumptions of male dominance.[8]

It would seem that a Church which is called to be *koinōnia* cannot fail to recognize and welcome the particular gifts of the female in the creating and nurturing of community at all levels.

Pat Collins CM draws our attention to the holistic, to that sense of connection and of interrelationship generally associated with the female, and essential to a communitarian model of Church:

> As modern Christianity slowly rediscovers the essentially personal and relational nature of its central doctrines, worship, and community life, women will become increasingly critical of the male bias of much of its institutional expression. I suspect that many men would be more comfortable with the didactic, ritualistic and dutiful characteristics of pre-Vatican II Catholicism. It is ironic, therefore, that leadership in the Church remains almost entirely in male hands. It is my belief that institutional forms of Catholicism will continue to decline until we switch from an overly male perspective, one that stresses separateness rather than intimacy, detached reason rather than felt thought, objective truth rather than subjective authenticity, action rather than being, the masculine characteristics of the God-image rather than the feminine ones. This will present a challenge of major proportions for male Christians. Unless they are willing to get involved in their own human development, and the challenge of relating to God through more intimate contact with people and nature, they will become increasingly alienated from the new forms of Christianity that are about to emerge.[9]

I have empathy with such insights because they speak to the heart of my own experience – along with all those with whom the stories have been told and shared down the years. Looking to tomorrow in a spirit of trust and of courage, and granted a true partnership of God's people at the service of a wounded world, what glorious stories are yet to be woven, told and shared along the pilgrim way?

NOTES

1. Avery Dulles SJ, *Models of the Church* (2nd edn; Dublin: Gill and Macmillan, 1988), p. 59.
2. Patrick Purnell SJ, *Our Faith Story: Its Telling and Its Sharing* (London: Collins, 1985).
3. Clare Watkins, 'Lay pastor: what *do* you do?', *Priests and People* (February 1994), p. 64.
4. Meeting of Latin American Bishops at Medellín; quoted by Margaret Hebblethwaite, *Basic Is Beautiful* (London: Fount, 1993), p. 19.
5. John Shea, *Stories of God* (Chicago: Thomas More Press, 1978), p. 9.
6. Quoted in *The Tablet* (2 April 1994), p. 418.
7. Quoted in *The Tablet* (23 April 1994), pp. 500–1.
8. *The Easter People*, p. 60, para. 178.
9. Pat Collins CM, *Intimacy and the Hungers of the Heart* (Dublin: The Columba Press, 1991), p. 119.

'To such as these the Kingdom of Heaven belongs'

children's spirituality and our contemporary world

DANNY SULLIVAN

IN ENGLAND AND WALES in the last fifteen years there has been intense change and development within the education system. The flaw in the approach to these changes and developments has been in focusing so intently on content. How children grow, develop, learn, their wholeness as persons has frequently been marginalized or simply ignored. To defend the integrity of children as persons, to recognize their innate sense of the religious and spiritual, to want to listen to them has been met in some quarters with the accusation of being 'loony'. Jesus, at least, was spared having to witness the worshipping of the national curriculum. The churches, to their credit, have tried in different ways to recognize the integrity of their children and young people. Yet, they too, have fallen into the trap of simply analysing children's needs and exploring ways of keeping them as part of the faith community. There remains a lack of courage and radical vision in understanding what our children have to teach us. This is not an attempt to set children up as perfect in some romantic or senti-mental way. Rather it is a plea to us adults to learn how to listen to our children, to have the humility to recognize that God is alive and active in their world and may indeed be trying to speak to us through them. If only we had the ears to listen.

If there is a theology of childhood it has much to do with a sense of story, of spirituality, of delighting in the Kingdom, of struggling to make sense, even at a very early age, of the harshness and pain of life. That theology appears to be lived in a natural and open way until children sense it does not reflect the world and language of adults. That is when they choose to retreat inside themselves and to hide their theology, their experience of Kingdom – sometimes to the extent that it remains hidden, never again to be tapped, enriched or developed through contact and dialogue with others.

A SENSE OF STORY

I was once working with a group of eight-year-old children who were preparing for their first celebration of the Eucharist. We were using the materials from *We Celebrate the Eucharist*, which had been inspired and devised by Christiane Brusselmans. Central to each theme in the material was an understanding of and the use of story. On this occasion the story was the call of Samuel. In my intellectual arrogance I expected that we would share the story and quickly find ourselves at the heart of its meaning. Such arrogance was abandoned as Elizabeth, one of the children, took us through her understanding of the story. She was captivated by the fact that Samuel could hear a voice but couldn't find the caller. This reminded her of playing hide and seek. It was exciting and it was fun. And this, she definitely informed us, was what God was doing with Samuel. Playing a game, having some fun, before moving on to more serious matters. Elizabeth laughed gently at us as she realized we hadn't even begun to feel the story. And that is what has remained with me to this day, courtesy of Elizabeth. That our stories are about our real lives if we only know how to understand them. That day Elizabeth taught me the value of the child as teacher and the adult as learner.

It is no accident that it was Christiane Brusselmans' understanding of the Rite of the Christian Initiation of Adults which led her to explore how best we can include children in the life and story of the faith community. The essence of RCIA relates to an understanding of initiation into the community. Thus the community has a responsibility to walk with those who seek to belong, to pray with and for them, to greet them on particular occasions and finally to celebrate their full admission in the richness of the Easter vigil. This journey of the adult seeker in faith is alive with symbolism and action. One senses that it was this deep human awareness and theological understanding that Christiane Brusselmans sought to bring to her materials for use with children.

Such an approach is affirmed and echoed in the *General Directory on Children's Masses*. This much undervalued and under-used document proclaims a whole feel of liberation in celebrating liturgy with children. It acknowledges how children grow and develop. It expects their liturgies to be 'convivial' and 'celebratory'. It understands the function of symbols, actions and movement. Critically, it recognizes that the experiences of children in liturgy at a young age will have a significant effect on how they perceive commitment and involvement in the faith community later in their lives.

THE PLACE OF THE PARISH

Our authentic Christian tradition is a story, which if fully understood, has the potential to transform relationships between people of different sexes, races, cultures, nations. In its unique way this story is dynamite. Children vibrantly understand the power of story and they have a facility for entering into it at different levels of understanding. The challenge to us adults is in understanding how we have transformed such a dynamic story so frequently into a damp squib of a tale.

One major mistake we have made with Christiane's materials on the Eucharist is to have reduced her human awareness and theological understanding into our obsession with 'the programme'. The 'rites' of the programme can become the order of the day as we work out how many monthly meetings will be needed to 'qualify' for the completed programme and access to the Eucharist. In some instances missing meetings would appear to be the new sin that has replaced missing Mass. This is a long way from a theology of the Eucharist to be explored and found in the gospels.

William J. Bausch in *Storytelling, Imagination and Faith* suggests that: 'The parish is the space and place in which storytelling and story healing take place for most people.' In the context of parish life in England and Wales and the religious potential of children Bausch's words would appear to be optimistic. John Paul II addresses the issue more realistically in *Christifideles Laici* when he suggests that we need to rediscover the true meaning of parish. To suggest rediscovery is to acknowledge that something has been lost. John Paul II refers to John XXIII's description of the parish as the village fountain. This is an attractive image – the fountain, where people can stop and gossip, meet old friends, and go away feeling refreshed and renewed in human terms. A real sense of belonging is generated.

Children have a sharp sense of what it is to belong. They have a real sense of justice. They understand the pain of isolation and bereavement. They tell lies without the refinements of adult subtleties. The reason they appear to be marginalized in the life of the Church is that many adults have lost a sense of the story which binds the faith community together. And the adults do not seem to realize what a rich resource they have in the children who are part of their community. We can tokenize them by allowing them now and then to plan or lead a liturgy, but we rarely have the confidence to nurture them in real ministry, to listen to them, to learn from their experiences and insights. So eventually they leave us in search of a story that will speak more to who they are. And we think they have lapsed!

THE PLACE OF THE SCHOOL

Children have not lost their sense of story and how it relates to all they feel and experience in their everyday lives. In the technological, media-obsessed society in which we live, the purpose and meaning of story can become marginalized – just as it can in the parish. An example of this in children's lives is the national curriculum for schools in England and Wales. Here mathematics, English and science have been iconized whilst art, music and drama have been edged to the periphery of educational life. School inspectors have found just as much evidence of this reality in Church schools as they have in other schools. The aesthetic, that which informs our thoughts and feelings, that which feeds our human spirit, which brings deep insight into the religious and spiritual, is not considered central to the development of our children as whole persons.

Here a different story is being offered to our children, one where utilitarianism is the order of the day, where learning is about knowledge and content. It is about mastering skills so that one becomes useful to society. There appears to be no space to celebrate what it is to be human, let alone to learn what it is to be. And our Church schools and our faith communities collude in this story if they leave it unchallenged.

Perhaps this provides an opportunity for those involved in teacher training in Christian colleges to proclaim an alternative vision of education rooted in an understanding of the Gospel. Whilst being aware of the constraints imposed by any government, there would be a wholehearted commitment to empowering and enabling students to become teachers with a sense of vision and mission. The depths of insight, the dignity and integrity of children would be recognized and affirmed. And all know-ledge would be seen to be in the service of that ideal.

We need to remind ourselves at times what we may be in danger of losing in our children. As co-director of the 'Children and Worldviews' research project I have often used story with a group of children aged seven to eleven years from a Catholic primary school. On one occasion I used the story *The Whales' Song* as a resource. Before reading the story I asked the children when they began to listen to it to hold on to the word, phrase or picture in their mind which spoke to them most. When I had completed the story I suggested they move the word, phrase or picture from their mind to their hand and clasp it shut. We then moved round the circle and as each child unclasped their hand we were told what they had been holding on to and why. This was done in a hushed manner and in its own way was spellbinding. At the end of this the eldest child present became quite agitated. Jabbing a finger at me he insisted that I make sure *all* children heard this story and that these children told it to their own children in turn. He felt that the story was too important to lose or to be left to chance and if it wasn't consistently told the relationship between whales and humans could be lost forever. This was a passion and an insight that we would be foolish to ignore. Within our Christian Churches we appear to fail to recognize this passion, insight and understanding in our children and when we do recognize it we do not seem to know what to do with it. This may be because we have lost the sense of storytelling and story healing for ourselves. The magic, meaning and excitement of story have eluded us.

Canon Francis Drinkwater, founder and editor of *The Sower* and a prophet in his time, wrote in 1951:

> To tell any story to listeners is a wonderful opportunity for the storyteller. And if it is a story that matters – like the stories from the gospel for instance – it is a great privilege and responsibility. First impressions, for better or worse, make such a difference.
>
> At the same time, for a story to do its work effectively there is not the slightest necessity for it to be new. Shakespeare never bothered to invent a new story – he knew that for catching the attention a known story was perhaps even better – so he took any popular story lying around and re-told it and how!
>
> Here indeed is the point – everything depends on how it is done.

Jesus was a gifted storyteller. He used the familiar and the known and he seemed to know how to keep his audience's attention. Christiane Brussel-mans understood this and in her own unique way tried to redirect us towards the treasure house that the Christian story is. Our failure has been to remain tempted into listening with the head and not the heart. Yet

Antoine de Saint-Exupéry's Little Prince reminds us adults that it is with the heart, not the eyes, that one sees.

A SENSE OF THE SPIRITUAL

A headteacher of a school for five- to nine-year-olds often used silence for the whole of an assembly. On these occasions the children, teachers and parents would come into the school hall in silence while music played quietly in the background. During the assembly the music would continue, there would be a display to catch the eye or sometimes slides would be shown. No words would be spoken and silently the children, teachers and parents would leave the hall.

It was after one of these assemblies that the headteacher felt her skirt being tugged by six-year-old Matthew:

MATTHEW	I liked that this morning.
HEADTEACHER	What did you like, Matthew?
MATTHEW	The quiet.
HEADTEACHER	What did you like about it?
MATTHEW	It made me think.
HEADTEACHER	What did it make you think about?
MATTHEW	About what I asked Mummy.
HEADTEACHER	What did you ask Mummy, Matthew?
MATTHEW	I asked her what being dead was like.
HEADTEACHER	And what did she say?
MATTHEW	She said it was like having a long lovely sleep.
HEADTEACHER	And what were you thinking this morning, Matthew?
MATTHEW	I was thinking, Mummy's right.

Matthew was involved in some profound thinking during his silent assembly and was fortunate in having an enlightened adult who enabled him to share his experience in a way that respected the integrity of how he was feeling.

Often we smile or even laugh at what children have to tell us. What we may be failing to recognize are the depths of insight and profound spirituality which may be opening up before us. Young children have a capacity for understanding the heart of things.

Kevin, who was five years old when his grandmother died, illustrates this point. Kevin travelled to Scotland for his grandmother's funeral. He experienced a tradition where the body was in an open coffin at the family home. On the day of the funeral the local church was full and the service lasted over an hour. Kevin also joined his family at the graveside for the burial. It had been a long involved morning. About a month later Kevin's Dad was reading him a bedtime story when he suddenly said: 'That priest who spoke at Granny's funeral was right. He said Granny was a kind person. So she was. She played games with me and she bought me those stickers on my door.' From the whole experience of death and burial of someone very special this five-year-old had taken the essence of who his grandmother was for him. How many adults would have managed to do the same?

Young children appear to have an innate sense of the spiritual. John Westerhoff III reminds us that children can 'sense the presence of God' and that they can 'imagine the Kingdom of God'. Children live in seen and unseen worlds and 'the Kingdom of God is first perceived in the world children know best'. Westerhoff is not attempting to idealize childhood and we must not. Children from an early age can experience pain, hurt, suffering and fear. Yet what Westerhoff sees as natural in children's lives is perhaps what Jesus saw as well. 'To such as these the Kingdom of God belongs.' Jesus, far from being put out by the presence of children, tried to enable his friends and followers to understand just what being childlike meant. They appear to have been somewhat slow on the uptake and we appear to have remained slow to understand this point ever since.

Robert Coles in *The Spiritual Life of Children* recalls the severe difficulty he had in persuading Hopi Indian children to speak with him in school. On the point of giving up, the school cleaner (a Hopi Indian) told him he was wasting his time. He needed to speak to them at home. When Coles did this he couldn't stop the children talking. They took him out to their sacred burial grounds. They explained why death was nothing to fear. They celebrated their faith tradition. The key was to value that tradition in the first place, which the school did not appear to be doing. We can make the same mistake in our own culture and environment. We can believe that children are empty vessels to be filled and not realize what a rich tapestry of spirituality may be already before us. We confuse being spiritual and religious with the practice of religion.

In the 'Children and Worldviews' research project we have, in a similar way to Coles, discovered a sense of children opening up about their religious and spiritual experiences only when they feel it is safe. For some reason they do not always feel it appropriate to share religious and/or spiritual experiences in the home, the faith community or the school. The danger for us adults is that we tend to make assumptions about the children's background and faith practice. We may use a language which relates to a formal sense of religious experience and practice but which in no way speaks to the actual experiences which children encounter.

In our research project V. told us how her Nan had prepared her for her death. She told V. what was going to happen and not to worry as even after death she would speak to V. in her heart. V. recalled to us that she remembered all that her Nan had told her and yes she spoke to her often in her heart. When life became difficult V. could always escape to her favourite wall where she would speak to her Nan who was in heaven and still looking after her and caring about her. V. had not explained this at school because she didn't want grown-ups to laugh at her.

B. was a youngster who was separated from his brother who now lived in Scotland. He missed him. His best way of coping with this loss was to imagine being with his brother. He did this when he played on the swings and soared his way to Scotland or on the rubbish dump when, out of the rubbish, he fashioned a boat that would sail from England to Scotland. He invited us to go on this imaginary journey with him, to meet the baby brother he missed so keenly.

It would appear that children learn to cherish and hold on to their experiences in ways that speak to them. If they find no context for them in the wider world in which they live, then they learn to adapt. Sylvia Anthony remarked in her book *The Child's Discovery of Death*: 'The child approached may close up, like a sea anemone or a woodlouse or he may display himself, like a lapwing when her nest is approached, who, of course, does not display her nest but cleverly conceals it.'

A CHALLENGE TO THE CHURCHES: INTEGRATING CHILDREN INTO THE FAITH COMMUNITY

If our models of working with children within the churches today are too closely tied to content and to adult thinking we should not be surprised that these children adapt and play the game according to our rules. What we lose, of course, is what Jesus suggested was a real insight into the Kingdom: children alive, alert and at peace with the presence of God.

Children have authentic values of justice and peace which our contemporary society desperately needs. Yet they may ultimately leave our churches if they find, as they grow older, no abiding sense of the values of God's Kingdom and reign on earth. If they journey further in search of that Kingdom perhaps we should not be too disappointed. All they have abandoned is the Church – not hope, the Kingdom and the presence of God! Herein lies our challenge. To listen to and learn from our children. We will not do this by locating the Kingdom in a building which is opened once or twice a week. Children know God better than that!

Christiane Brusselmans understood children, for she understood the presence and the Kingdom of God. Throughout her life and her work she strived to communicate a sense of integrity to the journey in faith that we all make. Story, spirituality and liturgy in Christiane's eyes were all one – an interrelated and integrated whole. She knew children would understand this because they lived it. It remains a challenge to us who would carry on Christiane's flame to strive for a recognition of what children have to offer us adults. We radically need to question our facility for putting them into comfortable boxes, for giving them attention at different ages and then forgetting them in between, for often offering them an experience of faith which they either don't need or, worse still, which fails to appreciate God already alive and present and active in their lives.

We either need to close our churches and learn what it is to build real community instead of maintaining a building, or we need to open, where possible, our churches to the whole community seven days a week. That way we may recognize that God's reign can be found wherever people are found. And there we may discover many of the children Jesus talked about, recognizing, in their own way, God present in their lives, in the midst of affluence or unemployment, materialism or poverty. We need to go beyond the buildings of our churches and learn to celebrate our Christian story in the cities, towns and villages where God's people try to live and make sense of the world. And we should not be too surprised to find God already present where we think God needs to be. And above all God will be amongst the children.

Children in our society and in our Churches have been marginalized. We do things for them, we give them knowledge, we provide them with schooling, with sacramental programmes. But we rarely listen to them or learn from them. Yet they are alive to the richness of story and to the profoundest sense of that which is religious and spiritual. To choose to consistently ignore this is our loss. Jesus gave us a remarkably short lesson about children but a lesson it was. One has a sense that he would have stood shoulder to shoulder with the ten-year-old in our research project who said with a sense of despair 'The grown-ups are not listening to us'. We grown-ups need to recognize with a sense of awe and reverence what John S. Dunne makes clear in *Time and Myth*: 'The child is there living with the unknown in the moment, playing as time itself plays with all the things of life in their seasons.'

Children come into contact with adults in a variety of settings – home, school, parish. In their own unique way they do not box and separate out home, school, parish unless we oblige them to. If and when we do this they quickly learn to adapt to our perceptions, our rules. Children's sense of story, their innate openness to the spiritual, the mysterious is a challenge to adults who are parents, teachers, catechists. Perhaps before we go developing yet more new programmes *for* children we need to rediscover and develop the childlike hidden deep *within* ourselves. That way we may begin to recognize the real meeting point for dialogue, for walking with and learning from our children. For: 'To such as these the kingdom of heaven belongs.'

REFERENCES

Sylvia Anthony, *The Child's Discovery of Death* (London: Kegan Paul, 1940).
William J. Bausch, *Storytelling, Imagination and Faith* (Mystic, CT: Twenty-Third Publications, 1991).
Christiane Brusselmans and Brian A. Haggerty, *We Celebrate the Eucharist* (Morristown, NJ: Silver Burdett, 1983).
Christifideles Laici (London: CTS, 1989).
Robert Coles, *The Spiritual Life of Children* (London: HarperCollins, 1992).
Directory on Children's Masses (London: CTS, 1976).
F. H. Drinkwater, 'Stories old and new' in *Educational Essays* (London: Burns and Oates, 1951).
John S. Dunne, *Time and Myth* (London: SCM Press, 1973).
Violet Madge, *Children in Search of Meaning: A Study of Religious and Scientific Thought and Enquiry Arising From Experience in the Primary School Years* (London: SCM Press, 1965).
Dyan Sheldon and Gary Blythe, *The Whales' Song* (London: Hutchinson, 1990).
John H. Westerhoff III, *Bringing up Children in the Christian Faith* (Minneapolis: Winston Press, 1980).

Servant friends

an experience of chaplaincy in a university college setting

PERRY GILDEA CM and JULIA HOULSTON

> No one has greater love than this, to lay down one's life for one's friends ... I have called you friends, because I have made known to you everything that I have heard from my Father. (John 15:13, 15b)

THE CHAPLAINCY

'To loiter with intent'; 'If you see a student, feed it'; 'To be a guide, counsellor and friend'; 'To help young people in their personal quest for meaning and faith' are all statements made by chaplains discussing their role in higher education institutions. Service, pastoral care, befriending and caring are the very heart of any chaplaincy work. In Britain the ministry of chaplain in higher education expresses itself in a rich diversity of forms. A residential college provides its own challenges and opportunities. Some of the things we say and do might not be practicable in other chaplaincies, and similarly the conditions in which other chaplaincies function will allow for different perceptions and expressions of this ministry.

St Mary's is a Catholic university college with approximately 2,500 students, of whom some 60 per cent are Roman Catholic and almost 30 per cent are Anglican. The chaplaincy team consists of three full-time members, a woman lay chaplain, a priest, and an administrative assistant. There is also a part-time volunteer helper, and the assistance of a married permanent deacon, who is a member of the theology faculty. The college has a new purpose-built chaplaincy centre, and a large college chapel in the centre of the campus. As the membership of our chaplaincy has expanded, and developed into a team, we have been working continually to fashion a common understanding and vision of Church, Christian vocation and ministry. We are very aware of the need for a model which springs from a good theological base. Such a theological grounding for this ministry is personally desirable and professionally necessary, especially in an academic environment.

1 INGREDIENTS OF THE VISION AND MODEL OF CHAPLAINCY

After the evening 'student Mass' on a Sunday early in the year a young student approached the chaplain, tears in eyes. She explained that although baptized Catholic, because of a marital split she had never experienced being part of the Catholic community in any way. This was her first time at a Mass: 'Suddenly I knew I was home.' She joined the RCIA and the following Easter with great joy made her first communion.

1.1 Community

The above incident is not unusual and illustrates the power of the worshipping community which exists in College. The college is fortunate in having a long history of strong community spirit. One of the most important functions of the chaplaincy is to further this spirit and underline its importance as an expression and experience of the Christian ethos of the institution. It is a starting place for learning that one of the most important experiences of Church should be as a community, a community which is called into being by the action of God in history, and sacramentally in the lives of each member; the community of all the baptized, the chosen race, royal priesthood of 1 Peter 9. The Pauline model of the body with its emphasis on unity of status (neither Jews nor Greeks, slaves or free, male or female), diversity of gifts and ministries is particularly appropriate (1 Cor 12:12–21; Rom 12:4–8). It is important for young people, many of whom are richly talented and with an open-minded faith, to see that gifts can become ministries for the building up and service of the community itself. Their gifts also enable the Church to fulfil its role as Christ's continuing, saving, presence in and for this world.[1] As chaplains we see ourselves both as part of this community, and as having a special responsibility for its development and mission.[2] The combination of community spirit with the openness and enthusiasm of young adults provides a unique opportunity to fashion a model of Church which incorporates many of the theological and pastoral ideas which are restructuring much of the Church today. It is our response to this opportunity which provides the following material.

1.2 Ministry

An essential aspect of understanding Church as living community is the acknowledgement of the reality of ministry as shared gift. This understanding combines an awareness of two aspects of ministry currently much discussed: ministry considered as institutional, the ministry of office; and the ministry which springs from personal charism. This perception arises from Vatican II's theological insight into the ministry of all the baptized and the ongoing theological elaboration.[3] For us this is not simply a bow in the direction of a theologically correct idea but an honest attempt both to understand and then to realize the implications of this insight. All must know and experience how they truly share in the ministry of Christ. What differs, as St Paul enthusiastically described, are the charisms individuals bring to ministry. The challenge is to discover the range of opportunities for exercising these charisms in true ministry. A chaplaincy team has a unique opportunity of being an expression and model of truly collaborative ministry. Hence the opening quotation. Each is called to serve the community according to one's gifts, and through the community the larger human family. All are called to a discipleship of equals, to a *diakonia* as friends 'to whom all has been revealed'. This vision is a challenge we must strive to address. The leaders equally are called to serve, to inform yes, but also to be informed, being open to the Spirit shared by all. This is not always easy and we will discuss practical aspects of the experience later. The starting point is the common baptism which constitutes the community, making all sharers in the one priesthood of Christ. The vision is of a truly organic community. Within the community the chaplaincy team is called to exercise a leadership role characterized by the qualities of service and enabling.

The challenge, excitement and difficulty of the ministry consists in working out the praxis of this vision and model. If we consider specific aspects of this ministry it will illustrate the process and our experience.

2 ASPECTS OF MINISTRY

2.1 Liturgy

In the tradition of the college, liturgy has been central to the work of the chaplaincy. We focus not simply on the actual worship, but on the preparation and planning necessary to develop and maintain styles and forms of worship which encourage the full, active and conscious participation which is the norm set by Vatican II.[4] The goal of the preparation and planning is to help the community express itself ever more aptly in worship and to encounter the sacramental presence of the Lord ever more fully.

On Mission Sunday each year we follow the CAFOD themes for worship. One year we combined two events. The theme was African. We invited students from the White Fathers, a pan-African group, to help plan the music and dance for our liturgy. Simultaneously, under the industrious inspiration of a former student, the whole community had been gathering and packing supplies for a village in Romania which has been adopted by a neighbouring parish. The supplies, every kind of food, clothes, medicines, and equipment from typewriters to fridges and wheelchairs, were stacked around the sanctuary. At the end of a moving and joyful celebration the congregation formed two lines from altar to door. Along the human chain were passed the collected goods, to fill a ten-ton truck backed up to the chapel door. All this was done to the joyful singing and the rhythm of African drums. This was truly a celebration and an experience of Church.

Such celebrations don't just 'happen'. The community liturgy preparation team meets each Tuesday to pray, discuss the readings for the following Sunday, and other special celebrations. These may be special prayer services, ecumenical or interfaith forms of worship, penitential rites or other special liturgies. In these instances the preparation team is always expanded to include the special expertise required for such different celebrations. The aim is to provide a rich, varied and ecumenical range of worship and prayer services. Such a concern is very important, as many of our regular worshippers are not of the Catholic tradition. It is important too to recognize the worship and prayer needs of other faiths.

Having prayed, listened to and discussed the readings, decisions are made on the special needs of a particular celebration. The preparation team includes those interested in music, drama, dance and mime. Depending on circumstances, each or all of these may be used if appropriate for a particular celebration. Because a close eye is kept on both the liturgical norms and pastoral need, the whole process is one of ongoing formation for all those taking part. The principles of liturgy and good celebration are regularly referred to, explained and developed. The leaders contribute liturgical experience and expertise, while others frequently contribute creativity, imagination and insight. The principal aim is to encourage the maximum participation in word, song, movement and silence of the whole assembly.

Recently we have come to realize the importance of involving those who will exercise the ministry of reader at forthcoming celebrations in the planning. The presence of the readers is important, as often too little proper emphasis is given to their ministry. The readers for a particular celebration can prepare and present if necessary the introduction, the penitential rite and the bidding prayers. Practices like this underline the importance of the ministry of the word, both for the commissioned minister and for the whole assembly. It also emphasizes the importance of diversity in liturgical ministry.

Eucharistic ministers are also represented or involved in the liturgical preparation. In their formation, the full extent of the ministry is emphasized. They are commissioned not simply to assist with the distribution of communion, but to bring the Eucharist to those who are ill, and to lead Eucharistic Services. The opportunity to prepare and conduct a Eucharistic Service is a very powerful sign of the real shift in the theology of ministry. Other ministers are those who prepare the church or a particular liturgical space, such as the sacristans, artists, dramatists. It is important that they, together with those who prepare the service sheets, greet the community as it assembles, take responsibility for the collection, are all treated as ministers, with charisms and gifts necessary for the good of the community.[5]

2.2 Ministry of social concern

Picture a cold windy December night in Piccadilly Circus or Leicester Square; then people the steps of Eros, or the space in front of the Forum Cinema, with a couple of hundred students. Half of these are enthusiastically singing Christmas songs and carols. While they noisily do so, the remainder cheerfully cajole passers by into contributing money for children in need. The infectious cheerfulness, the refusal to be daunted by weather, indifference or insult, their sense of life and fun, attract the local lonely and homeless. These over the successive nights become friends. Some return year after year. The students welcome them, feed them, treat them as human beings. This opportunity has been a conversion experience for more than one student, and a new start in life for some of the homeless. It is an unforeseen by-product of a fund-raising venture that has become a precious part of a long tradition. As for fund-raising, each year, in six cold nights, the students raise over £10,000 for children's charities.

This annual event, a community exercise *par excellence*, is one of the more important ways in which the college community expresses its responsibility to the needs of a larger community. The Church, the sacramental presence of Christ in our world, needs to look outward. We are fortunate that a number of college groups and societies exist which address some important social concerns. Some of these are sponsored by the chaplaincy and all are supported by it with practical, financial or moral help. The college St Vincent de Paul Society traditionally works on projects for the homeless, the unemployed, especially the young. Strawberry Hill Overseas Concern (SHOC) was founded to encourage alumni who wished to work in developing countries. It provides support and financial aid for projects in the areas where they work. Other organizations are concerned with the elderly and the disabled.

While much is being done there remains much to do. Students of the present age do not seem as politically and socially alert as their predecessors of fifteen or more years ago. One of the challenges facing the chaplaincy is to examine its own commitment to Church as social mission. Following that, it must engage in a process of ongoing conscientization of both students and staff. We have to develop a realistic strategy for devising effective ways in which the talents and energies of this community can be ever more successfully tapped in the service of the marginalized, oppressed and poor. It is only if our community sees itself as servant to the needs of the wider community that it can authentically unite itself to the sacrifice of Christ in worship, and in turn understand itself as a necessary and charismed member of the Body of Christ.

2.3 Ministry training

Ministry is not something that can be taken for granted. This applies not least to liturgical ministry. Lay ministry within liturgy is a powerful and convincing symbol of the rightful ministry of all the baptized. Therefore a considerable part of the endeavours and resources of our chaplaincy team goes into ministry training. Each year we try to further refine and perfect this process. In the coming year, at the opening liturgies of the semester, individuals representing each of the ministries will share the homily. They will speak on the nature of their ministry and invite the community to consider applying for one or more of these ministries. Over two Sundays they will invite others to share in both the liturgical and social ministries. As part of this process the chapel will be decorated with banners illustrating each of the ministries. Call is not excluded. There are always excellent people who are diffident about coming forward, who need to be invited and encouraged. The selected candidates will be invited to join a preparation programme. This programme will include a number of weekly sessions consisting in an introduction to the theology of ministry as it exists in the Church today. These courses refer to the past, to show how much of what is happening in the Church ministry today is a recovery of the good ecclesiological practice of earlier periods of the Church's history. They discuss the theology of ministry developing in the modern Church. It is pointed out that ministry is in the process of finding new forms of expression and ways to articulate its self-understanding. The instructions are also practical, dealing with the exercise and dynamics of the different ministries. The final stage of the preparation involves a residential weekend in a retreat centre where in an informal atmosphere of prayer and reflection the candidates are prepared for their commissioning. Commissioning always takes place at an appropriate Sunday Eucharist.

Some years ago we decided to experiment with our college calendar. We are a praying and worshipping community that is organic and integrated, yet if we adhere to the formal church calendar then the major liturgical celebrations are missed as community experiences, because students and staff are on vacation. We therefore introduced college Advent–incarnation and Lent–resurrection cycles. The last Sunday before the Christmas vacation is the day when this community celebrates the mystery of the incarnation. Similarly the spring term ends with a college celebration of the Paschal mystery. This allows us to fit an RCIA programme into a college community calendar. Our arrangement has incurred some adverse comment, and the accusation that it is sectarian. However, pastorally it is successful. The theological justification lies in the history of liturgy, which contains examples of local calendars and the disputes they occasioned.[6] It also helps us acknowledge that all of us live in a world with a multiplicity of, sometimes conflicting, calendars, and that the liturgical cycle is about the sanctification of human time. Our arrangement works by reinforcing the community aspect of Church.

We see the process of forming ministers theologically, spiritually and in practical skills as a most important aspect of our own ministry. It can offer an experience of Church which is both involving and challenging. Hopefully it makes available models of Church and ministry which will prepare young people and others for the future. In turn this may make them willing to work for institutional changes which will make this vision of Church more of a reality in the wider Christian community. It is therefore encouraging that some of our young liturgists and ministers are increasingly being asked to help plan and prepare important liturgical events at the diocesan level.

A serious gap in our present programme, and one we must address with urgency and creativity, is the absence of a training programme for the ministries of social concern. Certainly the community would benefit from the practice of a theological and practical training for these ministries, and a commissioning within the liturgy. Such a development can only enhance the self-understanding of the community as one called to exercise the mission of Christ as healer and servant.

3 PERSONAL DEVELOPMENT

We have described the preparation of students for liturgical and social ministries. An appropriate formation in Christian living and values is equally necessary. The challenge is to improve the ways in which we can help young people grow in their own self-awareness and spiritually. In the past we have organized a week of directed prayer during which each participant had a daily meeting with a trained director who guided them on a personal meditation journey. This was highly successful and we hope to repeat such efforts. For the coming year we have planned a number of retreats. Some of these can be used to introduce the participants to some of the currently useful methods of self-awareness, as instruments of self-knowledge and growth. This would include an introduction to the Enneagram, Myers–Briggs and similar programmes. Further mission evangelization addressed to the whole college community is planned. This would be conducted by an outside team since other voices may well speak to those whom the present chaplaincy team might miss.

4 A PASTORAL AND LITURGICAL TEAM

In the context of Church as a charism-filled community, one of the gifts of working with young adults is to be constantly challenged by them. Collaborative ministry means not only partnership of the leaders but being open to learning from all those who form our community. It cannot be enough simply to profess the presence of the Spirit; one must strive to acknowledge this presence, through an openness to the movements of the Spirit manifest in the lives of all in the community.

Like a parish we have a council, which we call the Pastoral and Liturgical Team. It is composed of the leaders or representatives of the ministry and concern groups already described. It also includes officials of the Student Union, and other college groups with whom we need to work or relate. Members of staff, non-academic as well as academic, obviously fall into this category. The number of meetings is limited for practical reasons but we try to make them as informative and businesslike as possible. It is now our policy that following the initial meeting of the year, the remainder should be open to all members of the college community. The model of a serving and open Church, allied to the concept of accountability, calls for such a practice. This forum is one of the places where we are endeavouring to develop in practice a suitable and authentic model of collaboration in ministry. We are aware there is much discussion in current writing of appropriate or effective models of collaboration and community.[7] This is an area in which there is still room for experiment and discovery of the most appropriate forms for this particular group.

5 COLLABORATIVE MINISTRY

The ideal we work toward is to model in our own ministry that which we profess. Our model should reflect the theology from which our convictions flow. In essence this model derives from an understanding of Church where ministry is shared, and the common denominator is the priesthood of all the baptized. In this short essay there is not room for an elaborate analysis of a theology of ministry. However, the key to our model is the current growth of awareness of the relationship between the ministry of the presbyter and that of the charismatic lay person who, it is now being recognized, is equally called by appointment and institution to share in the leadership ministry of the particular community. We must be committed to dialogue, openness, and working towards the discipleship of equals. The 'constitutional' situation means there are *de facto* differences of role in eucharistic and sacramental presidency. Apart from this present restraint everything must be done to highlight the rights and duties of the non-presbyteral leader. In practice, this means applying all the liturgical possibilities of leadership and ministry, particularly those elaborated in official documents,[8] and ensuring that all the other ministries are given full acknowledgement.

As leaders we must be committed to personal ongoing education, keeping abreast of the theological shifts and developments. We also must maintain a constant dialogue with those whose experience can illumine ways in which the full richness of collaboration in ministry and the development of the role of lay minister may be advanced. The very nature of chaplaincy work and, one suspects, the personality types of those who willingly come into this form of ministry carry with them heavy human weight. One discovers in myriad ways one's own vulnerability alongside an abundance of shared gifts. Collaboration brings with it excitement and promise, but also the inevitable reality of human tensions. These issues have to be faced and discussed in an open and frank way. New patterns of ministry require new models and methods of preparation and training. Traditionally the so-called ministerial priesthood is prepared for by a lengthy programme of study and personal formation.[9] Lay people are now coming in increasing numbers into pastoral ministry in their own right. There is still little in the way of organized, generally available, professional programmes for their academic or personal formation. Chaplaincy teams might be in a position to highlight the need and the content of such programmes.[10]

6 PLANNING AND PROFESSIONALISM IN MINISTRY

Towards the end of our first year as a chaplaincy team we spent a few days at a retreat house, first to dream and share, and then to write a pastoral plan for the coming year. This valuable investment of our time produced a plan full of good things. There was, however, a very serious unforeseen difficulty. The content of our plan was determined by our perceptions of our ministry and the needs of the community we were called to serve. What we failed to take account of were our own personal needs or strengths. The result was we were often exhausted and dangerously close to ministerial 'burn-out'. Apart from the obvious physical danger of such a situation there was an equally important pastoral disadvantage. We were seen to be always very busy. People would often approach us prefacing their remarks with 'I know you are busy' or 'I won't take up much of your time'. We had to stop and ask ourselves: what model of Church and ministry are we in fact offering? We learned a very important lesson. Ministers must take professional responsibility for their ministry, which must include their working patterns and their health both spiritual and physical.

This lesson was not without benefit. We have realized the importance of professional supervision and support. Part of our support system is an expert facilitator who sits down with us, inviting us to re-examine our dreams, our theories, and the relationship between these and practice. Our current plan has just as much of the vision and dream, but is more rooted in practicality and includes set and fixed times of freedom, for relaxation and social lives, away from the actual ministry itself.

An equally important discovery was the importance of spiritual well-being. Each of us has a spiritual director. An annual directed retreat is part of our commitment to our collaboration in this ministry and to the ministry itself. As part of this essential strategy our daily timetable sets apart time for prayer and administration. In emergencies we can always be available, but it is good discipline both for ourselves and for others to know that we set aside time for administration, letter-writing, and prayer together, and that these times are important to us and ultimately to our ministry.

The role of chaplains can be a ministry that seeks to be truly collaborative, and in the setting of a university college community can offer a special opportunity for enhancing one's vision of Church. As servants and friends to the community we can pass on 'all that we have learned', attempting to live out a model that invites others to know and exercise the ministries flowing from the common priesthood of their baptism.

NOTES

1. In the context of shared ministry and the consequent perception of Church, William J. Rademacher, *Lay Ministry: A Theological, Spiritual and Pastoral Handbook* (New York: Crossroad, 1991), pp. 169–174, lists a number of key New Testament qualities of Church as community that call for partnership. The first of these is *koinōnia*, which he translates as partnership. Others include the Pauline image of body; the common discipleship of the baptized; the common possession of the Spirit; the common

possession of the priesthood of Christ; a common mission flowing from shared baptism and confirmation; pastoral collegiality of 'a community breaking bread together and sharing with each other, not only the bread, but also their gifts'. His final model is the Trinity as an equality of persons with diversity of gifts.

2. James D. and Evelyn E. Whitehead, *Community of Faith: Crafting the Christian Community Today* (Mystic, CT: Twenty-Third Publications, 1992), situate the Church as a community that fits midway on a social continuum between primary groups, such as the family and close friendship groups, and formal associations, that is, structural organizations with explicit rights and obligations. They also comment on the psychological and sociological perceptions of community. The first perceives community as an experience of belonging, sharing and being supported, the latter perceives community as a structure to be analysed (pp. 16–22).

3. The following are some of the key contemporary works: William J. Bausch, *Ministry Traditions, Tensions, Transitions* (Mystic, CT: Twenty-Third Publications, 1983); Paul Bernier, *Ministry in the Church: A Historical and Pastoral Approach* (Mystic, CT: Twenty-Third Publications, 1992); David N. Power, *Gifts That Differ: Lay Ministries Established and Unestablished* (New York: Pueblo Publishing Co., 1980); Rademacher, op. cit.; Edward Schillebeeckx, *The Church with a Human Face: A New and Expanded Theology of Ministry* (London: SCM Press, 1985).

4. Among the most important official sources are the Constitution on the Sacred Liturgy, the General Instruction on the Roman Missal and the Directory for Masses with Children; these may be found in a number of collections among which are Elizabeth Hoffman (ed.), *The Liturgy Documents: A Parish Resource* (Chicago: Liturgy Training Publications, 1991), and Austin Flannery OP (ed.), *Vatican Council II: Conciliar and Post-conciliar Documents* (Dublin: Dominican Publications, 1992).

5. We have two 'styles' of Sunday eucharistic celebration: in the morning a more 'classical' liturgy with a choir and cantor; the evening music is provided by a large and competent 'folk group and choir' and there is more regular use of dance, mime and drama. These two styles are not totally disparate. There is enough difference to create opportunities for alternative experiences of worship suitable to various spiritual and psychological needs.

6. If it was not for some of these differences and debates we would not know when some of the annual celebrations emerged as universal observations. One of the earliest and most significant was the Quartodeciman controversy of the second century, which bears witness to different calendar traditions reaching back to the Apostolic Church: cf. Thomas J. Talley, *The Origin of the Liturgical Year* (New York: Pueblo Publishing Co., 1981), pp. 5–13, and Adolf Adam, *The Liturgical Year: Its History and Its Meaning After the Reform of the Liturgy* (New York: Pueblo Publishing Co., 1981), ch. 1.

7. Norman P. Cooper in a very useful and practical book, *Collaborative Ministry: Communion, Contention, Commitment* (New York: Paulist Press, 1993), discusses a range of models for leadership and ministry organization. They range from the 'classical style', with an emphasis on authority and preservation of the *status quo*, to the 'semi-mutual style'. 'In the semi-mutual style of leadership, the burden of accountability rests on the individual. Joint planning makes the individual periodically accountable to the other leaders' (pp. 49–68). Other aspects of modelling collaboration are discussed by Bernier, op. cit., pp. 179–82. This also forms a major part of the discussions by James D. and Evelyn E.

Whitehead in *The Promise of Partnership: A Model for Collaborative Ministry* (San Francisco: HarperCollins, 1993), chs 5 and 6.

8. The same documents referred to above in note 4 are relevant.
9. One could wonder about the realism and efficacy of the intended goals of either of these aspects, in view of the actualities of ministry in the future. Much of the formation still being offered works to models increasingly out of sympathy with many of the pastoral realities of the Church of the present, never mind that of the future. The effect of this will be to produce a group of ministers who will feel increasingly alienated, or will alienate the very communities they feel called to serve. See the careful analysis of the situation by Bernier, op. cit., pp. 260–8.
10. There are a number of courses both academic and practical being devised and some of these have international reputations. Equally, much is now being written; the works of the Whiteheads already referred to in notes 2 and 7 are among the more important.

Insider–outsider | 15 |

sacramental theology through the eyes of
children and young people

JOHN LOGAN

THERE IS A MEDIEVAL FRENCH STORY[1] told of a young boy who discovered the skills of juggling, made an ample living out of this and became the favourite of the aristocracy. As time passed and the juggler got older he started to make mistakes and ended up following the path of a beggar. One night he found his way into a building where he fell asleep and was awakened by the sound of singing. He had found his way into a cathedral and the sound of Compline had awakened him. As he looked around the pillar he had been sleeping against he became transfixed by the statue of the mother and child. It saddened him that the child had nothing to play with and he felt that was why his face looked so sad. After the people had left, the old beggar went and stood in front of the statue and out of his bag he drew his golden juggling balls and in one last triumphant performance he juggled until he collapsed and died. When people came in the next day they were saddened by the old man's death, but amazed to see that the statue had changed. In the child's hand there was a golden juggling ball and the face was no longer sad but wore a smile of contentment!

OUTSIDERS

Our society is full of 'outsiders' to formal religion, people who feel that their faith experience does not conform to the perceived views of established religion. The old juggler was an outsider, he had a dynamic of faith that would have contributed so much to the experience of worship in the Church, but had to wait for the church to be empty before he felt able to use his gifts to express his faith. Just like the old juggler there are many that are considered 'outsiders', or at the very least perceive themselves to be such. To be an outsider means that you do not have equality of opportunity, and do not have access to the power structure of the particular faith tradition. In this article I will explore the theme of 'outsiders' through my own experience as a Methodist involved in inter-faith dialogue, drawing on my experience as a teacher and parent. I will argue that those 'insiders' who hold power need to rediscover a new ethic of justice which is particularly present in the lives of the children and young people I have worked with.

To be an 'insider' you need to feel and be able to operate within the often rigid framework of formal patterns of lifestyle and beliefs and to feel that the 'gifts' you are bringing are acceptable in the eyes of the particular faith community. The old juggler had a very important gift to bring, but he had to wait until the church was *empty* before he brought it. This experience is borne out time and again by those at the margins. Those who hold the balance of power dictate doctrine and dogma. They define the boundaries of 'acceptable' faith. Emily Culpepper in describing her own story in the deep South of America says:

> My church's support for segregation pained and infuriated me. 'Red and Yellow, Black and White, all are precious in his sight. Jesus loves the little children of the world.' I have clear memories of singing this song in my all-white kindergarten Sunday school class and being upset. I believed and loved that message and the interracial pictures showing one child of each colour laughing at Jesus' knees. (I did not then notice how white-anglo-saxon-protestant were the features of Jesus.) My church wanted these 'other' children to stay safely out in the mission field or to be included after the second coming.[2]

'Outsiders' are often in this position, not from their own choosing but because they feel as the old juggler, that their own faith-experience patterns are not legitimized within the rigid frameworks of established religion. The experiences of children and young people can, like the old juggler, challenge the accepted patterns of formal religion.

SUFFER THE LITTLE CHILDREN

The British Methodist Church has for many years been considering the way in which children and young people are affirmed within the life of the Church. Much discussion has taken place on whether or not children should be allowed to partake in the sacrament of Holy Communion. Traditionally, receiving the bread and wine had been reserved for those who had come into full membership of the Church. In 1987 a report was approved by the Methodist Conference, which encouraged the local churches 'actively to encourage the fuller participation of children in the Lord's Supper'.[3] It acknowledged the diversity within local congregations and urged them to think more fully about children's participation in the sacrament. Local churches were urged to consider their own approaches to the inclusion of children in the sacrament. The debate was not without controversy. For some it was the notion of being old enough to understand the meaning of the sacrament, of being 'prepared' and being able to enter in to the sacrament as a believer. For others the concept of Holy Communion was seen more, as John Wesley himself put it, as 'the grand channel whereby the grace of His spirit was conveyed to the souls of all the children of God'.[4] Meanwhile, the children within my own local church had a different agenda. They talked, at their own level, about the meaning of the event, listened to stories, role-played the Last Supper and decided for themselves. They put their hands forward to receive the elements. The celebrant could not refuse them!

They were not aware that what they were doing was a political and liberating action and yet what was being said in these very simple actions was in essence a gesture of defiance to the adult structures and constructs. My own children were at the time very young and they took the matter even further. In a car journey we overheard them triumphantly shouting the words 'Jesus Christ'. As concerned parents we naturally wondered what language they had picked up from the nursery playground! When we glanced around the picture was very different. Andrew had broken his sandwich into pieces and was re-enacting the ceremony, in which we were all then invited to share. It was a great and moving privilege and for me the experience brought a new meaning to the words of the prophet Isaiah:

> Then the wolf will live with the lamb,
> and the leopard lie down with the kid;

the calf and the young lion will feed together,
with a little child to tend them. (Isa 11:6)

Children, too, are voices from the margins. Like other liberation theologians they can challenge our dogma, examine our constructs and provide
fresh and vital insights into the world of faith. The words of Jesus, 'Let the
children come to me; do not try to stop them; for the Kingdom of God
belongs to such as these' (Mark 10:13), were not a piece of sentimental
rhetoric but a statement that challenged the social constructs of the time.
The traditional rabbinic teacher/learner relationship was being reversed
and the children were being given a rabbinic function. As if this were not
enough the disciples were told that it was only by following the example
of the children that there was any possibility of entering the Kingdom of
God.

TO BE A CHILD

What can we learn from children and young people? It is clear that in
seeking to understand the views of children we must be aware of the
psychological and sociological backgrounds of the children we seek to
listen to. When we listen to children it is important to respect the
framework within which they are operating. It is essential that we develop
an understanding which differentiates between the word *simplistic* and the
word *childlike*. To label experiences and ideas simplistic is to use our own
adult constructs and not to try and understand the world as seen by the
'insider', the child itself. The word 'childlike' requires an understanding of
the child's frame of orientation, it requires clear and careful listening to the
'insider' in order to move along the continuum towards the concept of
'childlikeness'. Jean-Marie Jaspard argues that 'the formation of moral and
religious attitudes is always a part of the concrete mediation of the relations
of the child with its environment, with its love objects, its identification
models, its rivals, and so on, and that, consequently, these attitudes are
essentially evolutionary'.[5]

Current practice in religious education does not seem to have grasped
this concept.[6] Its focus has been the inculcation of knowledge and has
relied little on the concept of meaning. The presentation of religion has
been stereotypical and has frequently ignored the variations and permuta-
tions that exist within each faith community. In essence it has operated on

a simplistic frame of orientation. This has partly resulted from a mis-understanding by those who are not on the margins of society, and who hold the power, about what it means to be a person of faith, whatever your definition of faith is. There is a widespread assumption by the power holders that if you teach children facts about religion, you are in some way upholding a common sense of morality. Perhaps it would seem more appropriate to look for faith in the old juggler, the liberating faith, instead of regurgitating the same 'facts' which in reality become meaningless in the experience of children and young people because they do not seek to meet their needs. I have strong memories of teaching about the Hindu Sacred Thread Ceremony, traditionally associated with the Brahmin caste, to a group of non-Brahmin Hindu teenagers. They were totally confused and could not relate to the ceremony, denying vehemently that it was anything to do with their Hinduism. What as a teacher I had failed to do was to allow them to share their world-view and sit and listen to their perceptions of their own faith. In our faith communities we so often pass on the teachings as we received them. We want our children to 'receive' the wisdom of our forefathers. What we don't often acknowledge is that for many children and young people the mother is by far the most significant conveyor of wisdom, and popular culture has an overriding influence on them. Consequently much of the accepted teachings of different religions are in their eyes irrelevant to their particular needs. For them the mother figure is absent from their perceptions of faith experience, and liturgy and ritual often have very little to say to our children and young people. Invariably we fail to allow children and young people to develop their own theologies, but try to place our own adult and by implication 'superior' theological interpretations, the 'truths' as we call them. Often this is because of our sense of insecurity that unless we impart all our wisdom, our children will no longer perpetuate the faith. I can vividly remember as a young teenager in a Methodist Sunday School being castigated for stating that I believed in reincarnation. As a defiant teenager, this confirmed my view that my Sunday School teacher was bound to be reborn as an ant! This is not to suggest that there should not be a shared understanding of what it means to be an 'insider' in a particular faith, but that there needs to be space to explore without the prescription of dogma stifling developing experience. The true role of the educator, according to Jaspard, is 'to be present to the child during its moments of crises, doubt, and so on, in order to help it to understand itself and to grasp the new values it becomes capable of integrating'.[7]

Children and young people usually have a strong sense of identity. They have a developed 'frame of orientation'. The following statements are based on two interviews on the theme of 'community' with groups of children from a variety of faith backgrounds, including a child whose parents were self-proclaimed atheists.[8] The first group of children were aged seven and the second group aged fourteen.

The group of seven-year-old children made comments such as:

> 'I like going to the Gurdwara, you get food, you get Indian sweets and Prasad, it's God's special food ... '
>
> 'We don't, we get a boring old piece of bread ... It's God's bread ... because he killed himself to give it to us ... so you remember Him ... we say our prayers so that God knows us and remembers us ... we have to have some bread each and pray for my friends saying thank you God for them ... '
>
> 'Going to church makes me sad because Jesus had to kill himself, that's why we have the bread and wine ... '

To many, the immediate reaction to these comments is that they are inaccurate and consequently need correcting or interpreting. If they came from adults they might even be branded heretical. What they reflect is the strong sense of community identity that the children held. When a similar discussion was engaged in with the fourteen-year-olds the community solidarity was equally as strong, but what was very clear was the varying degrees to which the teenagers were prepared to accept all the traditions and dogma of their faith communities:

> ' ... My dad was born a Muslim and his parents forced him into believing it and he ended up not believing. I don't really find that I need to have a religion, as long as I believe in myself that's all that matters ... I describe myself as a Hindu, Sikh and Muslim atheist ... '
>
> 'I go to the Gurdwara every Saturday. I have to go, it's something my parents make me do. I like to sit down, sometimes things will be going on and I like to listen to them, it's very peaceful ... '
>
> 'I don't feel any problems in being a Hindu here, because I get along with all my mates ... '

What emerges from these quotes and the wider discussion is a sense of inter-mobility between religion and culture on the one hand and, on the other, an ability to locate themselves entirely within their peer group, which is intercultural in mix. To the teenagers concerned these dual locational frameworks are often entirely compatible. On the whole this transfer process can happen alongside the specific faith community context, thus preserving the integrity of the individual, but equally allowing the children and young people to engage in a very separate identity. The frame of orientation is strong but has a much greater flexibility and intermobility than perhaps existed in previous generations.

NAMASTE!

The World Parliament of Faiths met in 1993 in Chicago. What was extremely significant was the diversity of people who met to discuss global issues through the eyes of faith. It was a remarkable achievement and raised the profile of inter-faith dialogue significantly. Its Declaration for a Global Ethic deals with many important issues and principles and has set an important global agenda.[9] However, as is often the case, it is the practical and local implications of such statements that provide the greatest theological difficulties. These issues, if allowed to, can challenge the very roots of our sacramental theology, our understanding of the Ultimate Being. The Hindu greeting *Namaste!* really means 'May that which is of the Supreme Being in me, greet that which is of the supreme being in you'. If we take this concept a stage further we begin to say that in acknowledging that there is a part of the Supreme Being in every living being, then learning to understand that part of the Ultimate in others can only enrich and develop our own understanding of the Ultimate in us. Such a conceptual mode of operating could lead to fierce controversy. To people of a particular faith this leaves them open and therefore vulnerable and so this concept is fiercely contested and rarely discussed in an environment where orthodoxy prevails and religious fundamentalism is flourishing.

In the classroom it is a different matter. Children and young people very often have an awareness of the transcendent in others and challenge the boundaries and claims of religious élitism. On the one hand children and young people in a multi-faith setting hold strongly to their own cultural traditions, but at the same time they often seem able to translate that experience into the context of another's faith experience. Let me give you an example. A group of twelve-year-old students were given a summative task to 'Design and make a banner that will help Christians to understand the meaning of the celebration of Holy Communion'. The results were interesting and two were particularly significant. The students showed an in-depth understanding of the symbols associated with the celebration. Through their designs and through the process of discussion they showed understanding, compassion and sensitivity towards the experience a Christian might feel whilst taking part in such an act of worship. They were young Sikhs, with a very strong and rooted faith background of their own. What was very significant about this experience was the transferability of their spiritual understanding, whilst still maintaining their own faith integrity.

NAMASTE, MR WESLEY!

It is claimed that liberation theologians have a prophetic message for our times. So what is the prophetic message being lived by many of our young people? I would suggest that part of their message is as follows:

1. We must begin to see the world through 'childlike' eyes, to look for the transcendent without the shackles of dogma and bigotry constantly weighing us down.
2. Children and young people have a strong sense of justice and injustice. We should learn from them how to say 'that's not fair' and to challenge injustice.
3. Children and young people often face conflict, are frequently the cause of it, and yet at the same time they rarely bear any malice. We need to apply this understanding to the whole life of the Church and particularly to our understanding of the concept of 'sacrament'.
4. We must be prepared to see the *Namaste* in others. For some this will prove immensely challenging, uprooting and questioning their whole being, but it is essential if we are to achieve a global ethic and understanding.
5. We can learn that it is still possible to preserve our own distinct religious and cultural heritage, whilst at the same time learning *alongside* other religious experiences.

Religious pluralism is creating immense challenges to emerging generations of children and young people. They are having to face up to the everyday realities of living and growing in a pluralist community. Their experiences are different to those of preceding generations. Theirs is the age of intercultural encounter, where Western society has to learn a new

ethic, based not solely on Christian principles, but on the cultural awareness and understandings of vast diversity of faith. They have a greater
reserve to draw their inheritance from, and as adults we have the duty to
allow them the opportunity to do so, by listening to and learning from
their perceptions and world views. Only then will they achieve 'insider'
status.

The boundaries and definitions of sacramental theology need to be
redefined in the light of these experiences. The concept of sacrament
needs to be more inclusive, gain a greater fluidity and flexibility and be
opened to the insight brought by other faiths and experiences of the
Ultimate and those who are often labelled 'outsiders' because we cannot fit
their belief patterns within our own. The simplicity of children and young
people can, I believe, lead us to a new and liberated understanding of the
concept of a sacrament.

NOTES

1. This story is beautifully retold for children in Tomie De Paola, *The Clown of God* (London:
   Methuen, 1979).
2. Emily Culpepper, 'The spiritual, political journey of a feminist freethinker' in P. M.
   Cooey, E. R. Eakin and J. B. McDaniel (eds), *After Patriarchy: Feminist Transformations of
   the World Religions* (Maryknoll, NY: Orbis, 1991).
3. Quoted in *Children at Holy Communion: Guidelines* (London: Methodist Division of
   Education and Youth, 1987).
4. John Wesley, *Letters*, ed. N. Curnock (London: 1909), vol. 2, p. 315.
5. Jean-Marie Jaspard, 'The relation to God and the moral development of the young child'
   in Christiane Brusselmans (ed.), *Toward Religious and Moral Maturity* (Morristown, NJ:
   Silver Burdett, 1980).
6. A good example of this is the new model syllabuses for religious education published by
   the School Curriculum and Assessment Authority in 1994.
7. Jaspard, op. cit.
8. From an earlier article by John Logan, 'I go to the Gurdwara . . . I go to the temple . . . I
   go to Alton Towers', *RE Today* (Spring 1992).
9. Hans Küng and Karl-Josef Kuschel (eds), *A Global Ethic: The Declaration of the Parliament of
   the World's Religions* (London: SCM Press, 1993).

Epilogue: prophecy and suffering

> There is a fire burning in my heart
> imprisoned in my bones ...
>
> (Jer 20:9)

THESE WORDS of the prophet Jeremiah – surely a figure who knew what it meant to suffer in proclaiming the word! – express so much about the life and witness of Christiane Brusselmans. The fire with which she spoke never failed to enkindle responsive sparks in her audiences, be these church congregations, university audiences, or parish communities. She sparked audiences to laughter, singing – and always rapt attention. But afterwards, to an enthusiasm for prayer, theology, community-building, always with a renewed confidence in our own human experience and vocation to be educators in faith. She shared her story in such a way as to enable listeners to discover and reflect on their own. That same fire drove her around the world, tirelessly speaking, sharing insights, empowering others to build community. Always in the forefront of renewal, she was quick to grasp and act on the priorities of the time, and then move on to the next stage. It was her availability to people, not only for the lecture, or the prestigious seminar, but for the small intimate celebrations of family life and friendship, her sense of hospitality – her house was both symbol of and in reality a place of warmth and welcome – which make the pain and sorrow of her going so intense.

In her own prophetic role Christiane enabled and empowered ordinary people to discover their roots as truly the 'Pilgrim People of God', as truly an expression of local church with full sacramental expression. These roots had little to do with hierarchical power and status: instead she directed us towards a sense of those who were powerless in the Church – to women, to mothers and to children. Hers was a vision and interpretation of the Kingdom of God as the place where the powerless receive dignity and consecration to their true vocation.

But it is this vocation and mission which the Church found difficult to live with. During her life – despite her profound love of the Church – she never received the affirmation she deserved. Karl Rahner in his last book before his death spoke of the Church being in a winter-time. Through the renewal which Vatican II brought, Christiane lived through the hopes of a spring-time, only to realize that summer would not blossom and that we moved inexorably towards winter again. Yet it is the authentic toilers in the vineyard who are willing to bear witness – the candles are still burning! – and to keep alive the hope of a new flowering of the Gospel. The Second Vatican Council itself was only possible because of those who, for the thirty or forty years prior to it, had kept the flame alive, despite being marginalized, silenced and excluded.

We will never know the depth of Christiane's personal suffering, both the suffering which her personality brought, her illness, and that which she experienced in the institutional Church and her different work situations. Like Jeremiah and like Jesus, who, in the spirit of Jeremiah, cried 'I have come to bring fire to the earth – how I wish it was blazing already!' (Luke 12:49), Christiane had to confront opposition, marginalization and doubts as to her chosen path. We know that she encountered and struggled with loneliness, isolation and despair. Like Jesus in the desert, and alone on the mountain, she wrestled with her own humanity, her sense of inadequacy and fear. Jean Vanier writes that we are all broken people – and the only problem is that we flee this truth about ourselves. We follow stunted models of holiness which prevent us from discovering humanity in both its vulnerability and its fullness as *imago Dei*, or we adopt the trendy false gods of youth, money, 'beauty' – with all the effort spent on its attainment – and success. Let us not fall prey to a glorification of suffering. Jeremiah, Jesus and all who follow them as compassionate beings, 'bearing up the pain of God in the world', are called to resist structural injustice – including the injustice peculiar to religious institutions – and to strive for healing of body and mind. There's no great glory in being poor, says Tevye the milkman in *Fiddler on the Roof* – or sick, or unemployed, or homeless. But it is precisely from these broken places that our lives may be opened up to many people. Without our realizing, the Gospel message is opened up for others far beyond our knowing. In her darkness and pain Christiane became a symbol of the kenotic Christ: no glory, no fame, stripped of the magnetic enthusiasm which endeared her to so many. And, at the end, no angel came . . .

Will the Church ever learn from its prophets and their suffering? Will it learn the humility to accept their uncomfortable words, their disturbing gifts? Can it accept the truth which Paul uttered so long ago, that we have this treasure in earthen vessels, that we are flawed crystal, seeing through the glass darkly, but that from this brokenness can spring the fire which transforms, and energizes the tepidity, the lukewarmness against which the book of Revelation warns?

For Christiane there is now the light of resurrection far beyond the brokenness and pain. And knowing she is with God, we, her friends, can *keep those candles burning*:

> The shadows fall. The stars appear, the birds begin to sleep. Night embraces the silent half of the earth. A vagrant, a destitute wanderer with dusty feet, finds his (her) way down a new road. A homeless God, lost in the night, without papers, without identification, without even a number, a frail expendable exile lies down in desolation under the sweet stars of the world and entrusts Himself to sleep.

From Thomas Merton, 'Hagia Sophia'
in *Emblems of a Season of Fury*

Mary Grey

The contributors

Catherine Dooley

Sr Catherine Dooley is a Sinisinawa (WI) Dominican Sister who is an associate professor in the Department of Religion and Religious Education at the Catholic University of America, Washington, DC. Sr Kate holds a PhD from the Catholic University of Leuven, Belgium. She has published widely in catechetical and liturgical journals and has written a number of texts and resource materials for religious education. Her most recent publication is *To Listen and Tell: Commentary on the Introduction to the Lectionary for Masses with Children* (Washington, DC: Pastoral Press, 1993).

Perry Gildea and Julia Houlston

Perry Gildea CM and Julia Houlston are the full-time chaplains at St Mary's University College, Strawberry Hill, Middlesex. Perry Gildea has master's degrees in systematic theology and liturgical studies and a doctorate in moral and pastoral theology. He taught moral theology at All Hallows in Dublin and then was appointed as Spiritual Director to St Patrick's College, Maynooth. Following a period as senior lecturer in Christian ethics, liturgy and sacramental theology, he is at present leader of the college chaplaincy team.

Julia Houlston is the first lay chaplain at St Mary's. She previously worked as Catholic Youth Officer for Wales, and as Youth Development Education Officer for CAFOD in the Archdiocese of Cardiff. She is currently studying for her master's degree in pastoral ministry at Boston College, USA.

Mary Grey

Mary Grey is the Southampton University Professor of Contemporary Theology, based at LSU College, Southampton. From 1989 to 1993 she was Professor of Feminism and Christianity at the Catholic University of Nijmegen, the Netherlands. Publications include *Redeeming the Dream* (London: SPCK, 1989) and *The*

173

Wisdom of Fools? Seeking Revelation for Today (SPCK, 1993). She is editor of *Theology in Green*.

ANDRÉE HEATON

Andrée Heaton has been engaged in theological and religious education for many years at LSU College and is currently Head of the theology department, where she has encouraged the development of an increasingly varied range of courses designed to promote theological understanding and professional expertise in religious education. She has specialized in the study of worship and liturgy, which she has pursued not only in the academic forum but also through first-hand experience of pastoral work in inner London and the promotion and delivery of sacramental programmes in the parish setting. She is particularly interested in the relationship between models of communities of believers and patterns of worship in the wider context of faith and justice.

ANNE F. KELLY

Anne F. Kelly is a graduate of Mater Dei Institute and has a post-graduate degree in theology from Maynooth. She is at present lecturer in religious studies at St Patrick's College, Drumcondra, Dublin, and is a frequent contributor to journals, periodicals and other collections. She is co-editor of *Womanspirit*, the Irish journal of feminist spirituality. Recent publications include contributions to *In the Light of Christ: Old Testament Readings at the Easter Vigil*, ed. Brian Magee CM (Dublin: Veritas, 1994), *Death and New Life: Pastoral and Theological Reflections*, ed. Donal Harrington (Dublin: Dominican Publications, 1993), and *Religion and Culture in Dialogue: A Challenge for the Next Millenium*, ed. Dermot A. Lane (Dublin: Columba Press, 1993).

ANGELA M. LAWRENCE

Angela M. Lawrence was a lecturer at Maria Assumpta College in London. Subsequently she became Adult Education Adviser in the diocese of Arundel and Brighton. She has been invited to the Cook Islands in 1995 to spend six months giving leadership to lay formation and ministry.

JOHN LOGAN

John Logan is a senior lecturer in religious education at LSU College, Southampton. He has taught religious education in a number of secondary schools and more recently was Advisory Teacher in the multi-cultural London Borough of Hounslow. He is actively involved in his local Methodist church and is married with two children.

DAMIAN LUNDY

Damian Lundy is a De La Salle Brother now based in Oxford. He has been active in religious education at secondary, tertiary and adult levels, and has worked in many English-speaking countries both in religious education and as a retreat director, specializing in youth ministry. Between 1988 and 1992 he worked for the Bishops' Conference of England and Wales as a co-ordinator of the National Project of Catechesis and Religious Education. In 1990 he was awarded a PhD from the University of Manchester for his thesis on 'Adult catechesis in the Roman Catholic Church in Britain since the Second Vatican Council'.

ENDA MCDONAGH

Enda McDonagh is Professor of moral theology at St Patrick's College, Maynooth, Ireland. His recent publications include *The Gracing of Society* (1990) and (ed.) *Survival or Salvation? A Second Mayo Book of Theology* (1994). He participated in the Senanque Conference, 'Towards Moral and Religious Maturity' (May 1979), organized by Christiane Brusselmans and James Fowler. His paper appeared in the proceedings of the Conference, which they edited.

KENAN B. OSBORNE

Kenan B. Osborne OFM is a Professor of systematic theology at the Franciscan School of Theology/Graduate Theological Union, Berkeley, California. He received his doctorate from the University of Munich, Germany (1967) and is the author of several books on the sacraments, a book on the priesthood and a recently published book on *Ministry: The History of Lay Ministry in the Roman Catholic Church*.

MARY BERNARD POTTER

Mary Bernard Potter SP, a former primary headteacher, is now Religious Adult Education Adviser in the diocese of Leeds, England. She worked with Christiane Brusselmans on the revision of *We Celebrate the Eucharist*. She is the author of *UK Resource Pack: We Celebrate the Eucharist* and co-author of other sacramental materials. She has shared workshops with Christiane Brusselmans for the introduction of RCIA into England and Wales, and is a qualified trainer for evangelization.

PATRICK PURNELL

Patrick Purnell SJ began working in religious education in 1966 as adviser to the Bishop of Motherwell, Scotland. Later he became National Adviser for Religious Education to the Bishops of England and Wales. He is the author of *Our Faith Story*. At present he is working and writing on justice issues.

SUSAN K. ROLL

Dr Susan Roll was born in Clarence Center, New York. She holds a BA in classical languages from Niagara University, an MA in pastoral theology from St Bernard's Seminary, and in 1993 received a PhD from the Catholic University of Leuven, Belgium, *summa cum laude* with a dissertion on the origins of Christmas. She is currently an assistant in liturgy and sacramentology in the faculty of theology, Leuven.

DANNY SULLIVAN

Danny Sullivan is Senior Lecturer in religious studies at LSU College, Southampton. He is a former primary school headteacher and Diocesan RE Adviser. He is co-director, with Clive Erriker, of the 'Children and Worldviews' research project, which is exploring the whole area of children's religious and spiritual development. He is editor of *The Merton Journal*, the journal of the Thomas Merton Society of Great Britain and Ireland.

JOHN SUTCLIFFE

The Rev. Dr John Sutcliffe is Director of the Manchester Christian Institute and a tutor in the Northern Federation for Training in Ministry. Prior to this he has served in two United Reformed Church congregations, been Education Secretary of the URC and Higher Education and then General Secretary of the Christian Education Movement. His publications have included *Learning Community* and *Learning and Teaching Together*, and the editing of *The Dictionary of Religious Education*. He has been a visiting lecturer in Nicaragua and on several occasions in India, and a visiting professor in India.